TRIBAL FOLKLORE

ABOUT COUNCIL OF ANALYTICAL TRIBAL STUDIES (COATS) KORAPUT, ODISHA

COATS is a premier Research-*cum*-Academic Institute in the field of Tribal Studies. It is affiliated to Berhampur University, Odisha. COATS is a Registered Body under Societies Registration Act of 1860 bearing Registration No. 712/82 of 1991-92. It is situated in Koraput town in the district of Koraput, Odisha which is the heart of central tribal belt of the country.

COATS mainly aims at acquainting and educating the students, scholars and development workers about the tribal life, culture and development programmes. Presently, it imparts M.A. and M.Phil. courses in 'Tribal Studies' and its academic staff guide research scholars who are doing research leading to M.Phil. and Ph.D. degrees in tribal affairs. The Institute also undertakes District Planning and other evaluation studies entrusted by Central and State Governments. It organizes seminars, workshops and training programmes from time to time.

About the Author

Dr. Jagannath Rath is presently working as a Senior Lecturer in Economics in Laxmipur College, Laxmipur (Koraput District) of Odisha. Though teaching Economics is his profession, but research on tribal economy, society, culture and tradition is his passion. Being the son of the soil, he is more accustomed with the culture and tradition of tribes of Koraput region. He is well versed with languages of Kuvi (Kandha), Paraja and Jhodia Paraja etc. He has completed his Post Graduation from Ravenshaw College, Cuttack, M.Phil. in Tribal Studies from COATS, Koraput, and Ph.D. degree from Berhampur University, Berhampur. His Ph.D. dissertation topic is "Poverty and Trends of Exploitation among the Tribals: A Case Study of Kandhas in Koraput District of Orissa". He has published a number of research articles on tribal culture, economy and problems in reputed journals of the state.

TRIBAL FOLKLORE
A Study on Kuvis (Kandhas) of Koraput

Jagannath Rath

Published for
Council of Analytical Tribal Studies (COATS)
Koraput
by
CONCEPT PUBLISHING COMPANY PVT. LTD.
NEW DELHI - 110 059

ISBN-13 : 978-93-86682-92-5

First Published 2019

Published and Printed by

Concept Since 1974

Concept Publishing Company Pvt. Ltd.
A/15-16, Commercial Block, Mohan Garden
New Delhi-110059 (India)
T: 25351460, 25351794
E: publishing@conceptpub.com, W: www.conceptpub.com

Cataloging in Publication Data--Courtesy: D.K. Agencies (P) Ltd. <docinfo@dkagencies.com>

Rath, Jagannath, author.
Tribal folklore : a study on Kuvis (Kandhas) of Koraput / Jagannath Rath.
pages cm
Includes bibliographical references and index.
ISBN 9789386682925

1. Kandh (Indic people)--India--Koraput (District)--Folklore. 2. Kandh (Indic people)--India--Koraput (District)--Social conditions. 3. Kandh (Indic people)--India--Koraput (District)--Economic conditions. I. Council of Analytical Tribal Studies (India) II. Title.

LCC DS432.K192R38 2019 | DDC 305.894824 23

Dedicated to

Late Professor (Dr.) Krishna Kumar Mohanti

(21st March, 1940 – 25th January, 2017)

A Renowned Scholar of Anthropology and Tribal Studies

FOREWORD

The tribes constitute an important segment of Indian population. Even though they are said to be the aboriginals and indigenous people, still they have a rich culture. Their cultural heritage is quite high. The tribal people express their cultural identity in their social and political organizations, language, rituals and festivals, dress pattern, ornaments, technology, art and craft. They have mostly a folk culture. But there are a lot of finer values and positive things in tribal culture, which are worth preserving.

The Khandha form the largest group among the 62 tribes in Odisha with a population of 16,27,486 as per 2011 Census. They are mainly divided into two linguistic groups, 'Kui' and 'Kuvi'. The Kutia Kandha who mainly inhabit in Kandhamal district of Odisha speak Kui dialect, while "Kuvi" is spoken by the Kandha living the eastern part of Koraput region (undivided Koraput district). The writer of this book while using the term 'Kuvi' refers to the Khandha tribe living in Koraput district and who speak Kuvi dialect. He admits that, during his field study these people introduced themselves as the 'Kuvi'. They feel proud to be called as "Kuvi" instead of "Kandha".

Folklore is the rich oral literature of the tribal community. It is the mirror of their culture. It covers folktales, myths, legends, folk songs, riddles, proverbs, folk speeches and stories. It is the unwritten record of their cultural life. One finds a lot of positive human values in various aspects of tribal folklore and tribal culture. The tribal art, dance, song and music have greatly enriched the composite culture of Indian national life. They are the only people who can sing freely while working. They sing and dance in the forests, fairs, rites and festivals. They also sing and dance in the evening hours either in the village streets or in front of the youth dormitories. The tribals' sense of beauty and art is found in their wall paintings, wood carvings, weaving of clothes, ornaments and garments. They use specific plants and herbs having medicinal value to cure diseases.

The tribals love their villages, surroundings, eco-structures, hills and hill streams, countless flowers in the forests, their own people, songs and dances. They share everything in their community life. The joy and sorrow of one individual becomes the joy and sorrow of the whole community. One finds cooperative support in socio-economic activities of the tribals. In the tribal community an individual stands for the community and community comes to the rescue of an individual in times of need.

There is generally no fear of theft and robbery in tribal society. Their houses are mostly kept open, even when there is nobody at home. Their houses are as open as their hearts and souls. They have respect for dignity of labour. They hate begging. They work hard to maintain their livelihood. One finds rarely a tribal begging on the street.

The tribals, though generally poor, are very hospitable. They show hospitality to their friends, relatives and even outsiders staying temporarily in their villages. A high status is assigned to women in tribal culture. There is no dowry system in tribal community. Rather a bride price or "*Jholla*" is given to the parents of the girl before accepting her in marriage. Youth dormitories (*Dhangada* and *Dhangidi Basa*) were the core of tribal culture till recently. These are the places of social gatherings, cultural centres, place for entertainments, and places to select life partners. Folklores in the form of songs, dances, storytelling, and riddles etc. were expressed in the dormitories.

All the tribal communities not only possess rich cultural heritage, but also have unique traditional system of social control, in the form of their traditional Panchayats. These institutions exercise enormous amount of social, moral, religious, economic and political control over these communities.

The discipline in social life, dignity of labour, the collective and cooperative support in socio-economic activities, love and respect for trees and forests, their songs, music, dance, ornaments, arts and crafts hospitality and exchange of gifts and their simplicity etc. are the positive aspects which may be properly channalised for promoting their sustainable development.

Kandhas are not only the largest tribal group in Odisha, but also they have a rich folk culture. Their folklore or unwritten literature like that of tribal communities elsewhere contains valuable human values. Dr. Jagannath Rath, the author of the book, though a non-tribal, hails from a Kandha dominated area of Koraput region and he has good command over Kandha (Kuvi) dialect. He has tried to focus on the Kandha culture, both material and non-material, while dealing with their folklore aspects. He has collected some of the folk aspects of the

Kuvis (Kandhas) through their myths, proverbs, songs, stories etc. and specifically tried to highlight socio-economic and religious importance and human values contained in them. Sincere efforts are needed to document and record these valuable folk literatures of the tribals in general and that of Kuvis (Kandhas) in particular. It is, because, they not only have great socio-economic and religious importance but also contain a lot of human values.

It is hoped that this piece of research output of the scholar on Kuvi (Kandha) culture in general and their folklore in particular will provide intellectual feedback to the academicians, scholars, and others who are interested to know about the tribal culture, particularly their folklores.

Dr. Jagabandhu Samal
Professor
Council of Analytical
Tribal Studies (COATS)
Sabara Shreekshetra
DNK Road, Koraput
Odisha – 764020

Books from Council of Analytical Tribal Studies (COATS), Koraput, Odisha

Sl.No.	Title of the Book	Editors/Authors/Publishers
1.	Forest Management in Tribal Areas	P.M. Mohapatro & P.C. Mohapatro (Ed.) Concept Publishing Company (P) Ltd., New Delhi (1997)
2.	AmoGaon O AmoSasan (Odia)	J. Samal & N.N. Pradhan (Ed.) Hindustan Offset Printers, Jeypore, Koraput (2002)
3.	Dongar Katha (in Odia)	J. Samal Hindustan Offset Printers, Jeypore, Koraput (2002)
4.	Organisation and Management of Tribal Markets	K.K. Behera Independent Publishing Company, Delhi (2003)
5.	Tribes of Koraput	K.K. Mohanti P.C. Mohapatro & J. Samal Hindustan Offset Printers, Jeypore, Koraput (2006)
6.	Sustainable Development in Bonda Hills	P.M. Mohapatro K.K. Mohanti & P.C. Mohapatro Perfect Print and Graphics, Bhubaneswar (2009)
7.	Didayi — The Primitive Tribe	Gopinath Pradhan Hindustan Offset Printers, Jeypore, Koraput (2009)
8.	Law Preventing Land Alienation by Scheduled Caste and Scheduled Tribe	Jagannath Shorff Concept Publishing Company (P) Ltd., New Delhi (2013)
9.	Participatory and Sustainable Development among the Didayi	P.M. Mohapatro K.K. Mohanti & P.C. Mohapatro (Ed.) Concept Publishing Company (P) Ltd., New Delhi (2014)
10.	Shifting Cultivation in India — A Tribal Livelihood Alternative	N.K. Rath Concept Publishing Company (P) Ltd., New Delhi (2015)
11.	Watershed Management — Effective Tool for Sustainable Livelihood	A.K. Mohanty Concept Publishing Company (P) Ltd., New Delhi (2017)

PREFACE

Adibasis (tribals) have an unwritten or oral literature. It is called "Folklore". It covers folktales, myths, legends, folk songs, riddles, proverbs, folk speeches, stories, folk dances, arts and crafts. It is the unwritten record of their cultural life, which has been transmitted from one generation to another. The folklores of these simpler society have socio-economic and religious importance. These also contain high human values. Not only it reflects the culture of the tribal community but also brings solidarity, continuity and consistency among the group.

This book is the outcome of a research study on tribal folklore with special emphasis on Kuvis or Kandhas. The Kandhas residing in Odisha are divided into two linguistic groups, i.e. "Kui" and "Kuvi". "Kui" dialect is spoken by the Kutia-Kandhas mostly living in Kandhamal district. Kuvi is mainly spoken by the Kandhas in the eastern part of Koraput region. The later section of the Kandha feel proud to be identified as "Kuvi" as ascertained by the author through his close contact with them. Hence, the term "Kuvi" is used in place of Kandha in this book.

While, studying the folklore aspects of the Kuvis, special interest has been made to find out socio-economic and religious importance contained in such oral literature as well as the human values in them.

This book is the outcome of a research study at M.Phil. level which was undertaken under the guidance and supervision of Dr. Jagabandhu Samal, Professor, Council of Analytical Tribal Studies (COATS), Koraput. He is kind enough to write the foreword to this book. I humbly express my gratitude to him for his guidance and supervision both at M.Phil. and Ph.D. level.

I am also grateful to Dr. P.C. Mohapatro, Director, COATS, Koraput for his comments and suggestion on my work and encouraging me to complete the work. He also took special interest to publish the work in the form of a book.

I express my heartfelt regards and gratitude to Late Professor (Dr.) Krishna Kumar Mohanti, a renowned scholar and former Director of SCSTRTI, Odisha, Former Director of both NKCDS and ATDC, and Chairman of COATS, Koraput. He was kind enough to go through the manuscript in detail and he made necessary corrections before his heavenly departure from this material world on 25th January, 2017. He also advised me to publish the work with necessary revision. As a token of my deep sense of love and regards to this great scholar, I have dedicated this piece of work to him.

I am also thankful to the Principal and all my colleagues of Laxmipur College and staff members of COATS, Koraput for their support to complete my work.

I express my deep sense of appreciation and thankfulness to my students Mr. Ramesh Jambeka, Mr. Tapan, Miss Saibi Manding, Miniyaka, Miss Kasa Janbeka, and Mr. Kabish Hikoka and all other respondents of sample villages for helping me to collect information required.

I also express my thanks to my wife Sriya (Sabitree), loving daughter Shrim (Debansika) and son Shrit (Debashrit) for all those inconveniences they might have faced during my fieldwork. I am also grateful to my elder sisters Kuni (Jagyaseni), Titi (Mana Mohini) and Mami (Jagat Mohini) who have constantly inspired me to undertake research works on tribal culture and livelihood. Let, this book be a tribute to my heavenly parents Late Basant Kumar Rath and Prafulla Kumari Rath. Let they pardon me for not being able to compete this piece of work during their lifetime.

Last but not the least, I take the opportunity to convey my sincere thanks to Concept Publishing Company (P) Ltd., New Delhi who readily accepted the responsibility to publish the book and release it in time.

Jagannath Rath

CONTENTS

LIST OF MAPS

LIST OF TABLE

LIST OF PHOTOGRAPHS

ABBREVIATIONS

AOBRC	:	Andhra Orissa Border Regional Committee
APE	:	Average Per Capita Expenditure
APL	:	Above Poverty Line
BBSR	:	Bhubaneswar
BC	:	Before Christ
BPL	:	Below Poverty Line
CAPART	:	Council for Advancement of People's Action and Rural Technology
COATS	:	Council of Analytical Tribal Studies
CMAS	:	Chasi Muliya Adivasi Sangha
EGS	:	Employment Guarantee Scheme
FLR	:	Female Literacy Rate
FAO	:	Food and Agriculture Organisation
GDP	:	Gross Domestic Product
GP	:	Gram Panchayat
HAL	:	Hindustan Aeronautics Limited
HH	:	Household
HINDALCO	:	Hindustan Aluminum Company
HQ	:	Head Quarter
IRDP	:	Integrated Rural Development Programme
ITDA	:	Integrated Tribal Development Agency
IWDP	:	Integrated Wasteland Development Project
LAMP	:	Large Size Multipurpose Society
LI Points	:	Lift Irrigation Points
MADA	:	Modified Area Development Approach
MFP	:	Minor Forest Produces
MSL	:	Mean Sea Level
NGO	:	Non-Governmental Organisation
NIRD	:	National Institute of Rural Development
NREGS	:	National Rural Employment Guarantee Scheme
NSSO	:	National Sample Survey Organisation
PC	:	Percentage
PDS	:	Public Distribution System

PCI	:	Per Capita Income
PESA Act	:	Panchayats (Extension to the Scheduled Areas) Act
PHC	:	Public Health Centre
PLB	:	Poverty Line Basket
PPP	:	Purchasing Power Parity
PRH	:	Percentage of Rural Household
PRI	:	Panchayati Raj Institution
PTG	:	Primitive Tribal Group
QLI	:	Quality of Life Index
SC	:	Scheduled Castes
SHG	:	Self-Help Group
SJGSY	:	Swarna Jayanti Gram Swarojgar Yojana
SMPT	:	Special Multipurpose Tribal Development Block
ST	:	Scheduled Tribes
TD Blocks	:	Tribal Development Blocks
TSP	:	Tribal Sub-Plan
UGPHC	:	Up-Graded Primary Health Centre
UNDP	:	United Nations Development Programme
UNICEF	:	United Nations International Children's (Emergency) Fund
UPPL	:	Ultra Poor Poverty Line
URP	:	Uniform Reference Period
VHP	:	Viswa Hindu Parishad

1

INTRODUCTION

India is a vast country with geographical, political, cultural, linguistic, religious and ethnic diversity. Diversity forges unity and gives India her unique character in terms of cultural wealth. An important feature of Indian society is its stratified structure that organizes society into hierarchic caste groups, solely determined by birth.

However, there is another large section of population which falls outside the purview of the caste-based structure of society. This section is termed as Scheduled Tribes (STs) or "indigenous people" — a term that is widely used and accepted in international circles. In India, STs were popularly known as *Vanajati/Vanvasi* (forest dwellers), *Pahari* (hill dwellers), *Adimjati* (original inhabitants), *Adivasi* (first settlers), *Janjati* (folk people) and *Anusuchit Janajati* (Scheduled Tribes).

The present study is an humble attempt to know the folklore of the Tribals and its socio-economic importance. The author has particularly taken the case of Kuvis (Kandhas) of Koraput, Odisha.

Before going to analyse about the Tribal Folklore, it is better to know about the concepts like the Tribe and Folklore and their related features. This chapter attempts to define the terms like "the tribes" and "the folklore". Keeping this in view, the chapter on introduction is divided into three different sections. Section I deals with definition of tribes, their geographical distribution, tribal groups in India, Odisha and Koraput. Section II deals with the meaning of the term "folklore" and its genres. And Section III deals with a brief methodological perspective of the present study, which points out the objectives, hypotheses, methods and techniques, universe and sample, tools and field techniques used for this study.

SECTION I
Definition and Characteristics of a Tribe

Over centuries, a host of anthropologists, sociologists, administrators and social workers have put forward various definitions for the term "tribe" but the term remains obscure and it is very difficult to define the tribal population in terms of any single set of formal criteria because of the variation of the cultural and social values from one tribe to another. However, some of the prominent definitions are discussed below:

The Imperial Gazetteer of India states that "a tribe is a collection of families bearing a common name, speaking a common dialect, occupying or professing to occupy a common territory and not usually endogamous, though originally it might have been so."

Piddington defines tribes as "a group of people speaking a common dialect inhabiting a common territory and displaying certain homogeneity in their culture" [Piddington, R. (1956:164) *An Introduction to Social Anthropology*].

Hoebel defines tribe as "a social group speaking a distinctive language or dialect and possessing a distinctive culture that marks it as different from all other tribes. It is not necessarily organized politically" (Hoebel, 1949:513).

E.B. Tagor in the Dictionary of Anthropology defines tribe as "a social group usually occupying a definite area, with a dialect, cultural homogeneity and unifying social organization. It may include several sub-groups such as 'sibs' or villages. A tribe ordinarily has a leader and may have a common ancestor, as well as a patron deity. The families or small communities making up the tribe are linked through economic, social, religious, family or blood ties."

D.N. Majumdar defines tribe as "a social group with territorial affiliation, endogamous, with no specialization of functions, ruled by tribal officers, hereditarily or otherwise united in language or dialect, recognizing social distance with other tribes or castes without any social obloquy attaching to them, as it does in the caste structure, following tribal traditions, beliefs and customs and above all conscious of a homogeneity of ethnic and territorial integration" (Majumdar, 1958).

He opines that a tribe has a traditional territory and emigrants always refer to it as their home. Even though all the members of a tribe may not be related by blood to each other, kinship operates as a strong regulative and integrating principle. Politically, the tribes of India are under the control of the State Governments, however, within themselves there exist many self-governing bodies. Joint ownership of property and the presence of "dormitory institutions" are some of the unique features of tribes of India.

Ralph Linton defines tribe as "a group of bands occupying a contiguous territory or territories and having a feeling of unity derived from numerous similarities in culture, frequent contact and a certain communality of interest."

I.M. Lewis states "Ideally, tribal societies are small in scale, are restricted in the spatial and temporal range of their social, legal and political relations, and possess a morality, a religion and world-view of corresponding dimensions. Characteristically too, tribal language is unwritten and hence, the extent of communication both in time and space is inevitably narrow. At the same time, tribal societies exhibit a remarkable economy of design and have a compactness and self-sufficiency lacking in modern society."

The term 'tribe' has been derived from English term "TRIBUZ" which has a Latin root. The term means three divisions into which the early Romans were grouped. The meaning of the term varies from nation to nation. The Romans conceived the term as a political division, while the Greeks seemed to have equated the term with fraternities and in Irish History, the term means families of communities having the same surname.

The Concept of 'Tribe' in Indian Context

In common parlance tribes were usually taken to be highlanders or the dwellers of hills and forests. This notion, however, is not adequate to understand the tribes properly. Moreover, this type of approach is rather offensive one, as it implies that the tribes are nothing but hill people or jungle men.

Some anthropologists opine that the nomenclature "tribe" is a "colonial construction". They are of the view that the character of this group was consolidated by the British through the process of classification and enumeration. It does not mean "tribe", what we call today did not exist in the pre-colonial period, but that the British placed these groups under the category of "tribe". The terms "tribe" and "caste" were used as synonyms in writings of the eighteenth century and later as cognates in administrative and ethnographic accounts. The British treated the tribes as different from the rest of the Indian population and had different administrative set-up for the two. The administrative domains were termed as Scheduled Areas and excluded or partially excluded areas.

The criteria for identifying a group as tribal were often inexplicit and blurred. This is evident in the census survey carried out in 1881 when the term "forest tribe" was used under the broad category of agricultural and pastoral castes. Subsequently, the 1901 Census described them as "group which practised animism"; the 1921 Census described them as "hill and forest tribes" and that held in 1931 described them as "primitive tribe". Though consecutive census surveys attempted to arrive at definitive criteria for tribes, they were often either ambiguous or inadequate. In the writing of British, a "tribe" is referred to as a group claiming descent from a common ancestor or one which lived in primitive and barbarous conditions.

So, it can be said that the category of "tribe" was introduced in modern consciousness by British colonial rule. It was further consolidated by administration in the post-Independence era.

Post-Independence period literature on tribes was mainly derived from three sources — the Anthropological Survey of India, the Tribal Research Institutes established in the 1950s and Universities Departments.

In Anthropological literature, tribes were viewed as a composite society, more or less homogenous — with common language, culture, customs, governments etc., tribal societies were often viewed as one amongst many stages in the evolution of society. They were also viewed in terms of segmented features, in as much as tribes in spite of their limited spatial dimension and the temporal range of their socio-political and legal relations did possess a definite structure.

However, in Indian context, it is the administrative rather than the anthropological concept of tribes that exists today. "Tribes" are those communities which have been enumerated in the Constitution of India in the list of Scheduled Tribes. The Constitution defines Scheduled Tribes as "community or part of, or groups within such communities, as is deemed under Article 342 to be a Scheduled Tribe". So, it is evident that defining 'tribe' is based on enumeration and has little to do with the anthropological concept of tribes. It is found that there is a little scientific basis on which the categorization of Scheduled Tribes can be defended.

In the post-Independence period several concerted efforts were made to arrive at a consensus on the status of a group as a "tribe". In 1950, the Commissioner of Scheduled Caste and Scheduled Tribes sought the views of different regions and states regarding the criteria for defining tribes. The most common criteria suggested were, physical characteristics, linguistic affiliation, cultural contact, economy and ecological considerations. On the other hand, tribal dialects, animism, primitiveness, occupation, and living in inaccessible areas were also determining criteria used to define tribes.

However, the exclusion or inclusion of a particular group in the list reflects political mobilization rather than an anthropological notion of the same. It is lined to the extension of administrative and socio-political concessions to the groups concerned.

Thus, defining a tribe in the Indian context is not an easy task and there is no single universally accepted definition for the nomenclature "tribe". So, academically we are nowhere near a comprehensive method of identifying the "tribe", simply, accepting the ethnic group, identified by the Constitution of India as Scheduled Tribes. Singh (1982) points out in the similar fashion: "Any discussion of tribes in India has to proceed from the assumption that a tribe is an administrative and political concept of India."

Characteristic Features of Tribes

Standardization of characteristic feature of "tribe" is rather difficult. Still, we may see that a tribe is a social group of people who have the following nine features, *viz.*,

(i) A definite territory or who claim to occupying a common territory,
(ii) A common name,
(iii) A common dialect/language,
(iv) A common culture,
(v) A shaped behavioural pattern of an endogamous group,
(vi) Common taboos,
(vii) Existence of distinctive social and political systems.
(viii) Full faith in their leaders, and
(ix) Self-sufficiency in the distinct economy (Vidyarthi and Rai, 1976:167).

T.B. Naik tried to enumerate the criteria and indices of tribal way of life in the Indian context. He stated that "a tribe should have the least functional interdependence within the community, should be economically backward, should have a common dialect, should be politically organized, should have customary laws, should be geographically isolated and should have the least desire to change."

Tribal communities in India have lived along with non-tribal communities belonging to different religions and cultures for several centuries. Often, the characteristic features between the two overlapped and distinction blurred.

Tribes of India

As per the Constitution of India, initially 427 tribes were identified as Scheduled Tribes (Bose, 1971) and the number has gone up to 698 (including sub-groups) at present (*Draft National Policy on Tribals*, 2006). They are found mostly in 23 States and four Union Territories. The Scheduled Tribes have not been specified in two States of India, i.e. in Punjab and Haryana and three Union Territories, i.e. in Chandigarh, Delhi and Puducherry. Mizoram has the highest percentage (94.75%) of STs and Uttar Pradesh, the lowest percentage (0.21%) of the total population of the state.

As we saw, there is no single criterion for defining and classifying tribes in India. Different categorizations have been made of tribes on the basis of geography/territory, language, physical/racial attributes, size, economy or subsistence patterns and the degree of assimilation into mainstream society. They may be discussed as follows:

Distribution of Tribes in India

The tribes in India are distributed in varying numbers in different parts of the country. Their economy and culture have been designed according to the ecological conditions in which they live.

Geographical Distribution

Geographically, the tribes of India have been divided into the following geographical zones: The Himalayan region, Middle Indian Region, Western Indian Region, South Indian Region and the Island Region.

The tribes inhabiting the Himalayan region are the Akas, Daflas, Apatanis, Mishmis, Khamptis, Singphos, Kukis, Khasis, Garos, Lepchas, Bhotias, Tharus, Juangs, Kharia, Khonds, Bhumijs, Baiga, Muria, Marias, Mundas, Gonds, Santhals, Oraons etc. inhabit the Middle India Region.

Tribes inhabiting in the Western region include the Barodias, Bharwads, Bhils, Damors, Dhanwars, Dhodias, Girasias, Gonds, Katkaris, Koknas, Kolis, Minas, Siddis and the Warlis.

Tribes like the Chenchus, Irulas, Paniyans, Kurumbas, Kadars, Todas, Badagas, Kotas etc. inhabit the South India Region.

The Island Region is inhabited by the Jarwas, Onges, the Great Andamanese, North Sentinelese, amongst others.

Linguistic Distribution

Tracing the linguistic map of India, we can see that diverse groups of tribes in India speak different languages in various regions. Some of the language families found among the tribal communities of India are:

The Dravidian language family of tribes are found in southern India and in some pockets in central India which include the Gonds, Oraons, Kandh, Todas, Palligans, Irulas, Chenchus, Kadars etc.

The Austro-Asiatic language is spoken in some pockets of the north-eastern Himalayan region of Meghalaya, in Nicobar Islands and in most part of central India by tribes like the Khasis, Jaintias, Mundas, Santhals, Hos, Saoras, Bondos, Korkus etc.

Tibeto-Chinese languages are spoken in the entire Himalayan region. The Tai group of people (Khamptis, Phakials), Bhotia, Khampa, Memba, Akas, Miri, Lepchas, Totos, Mishmis, Nocte, Sulung, Tagin, Kachari, Dimasa, Garo, Lotha, Konyak, Hmar, Koireng, Paite; Vaiphei, use this family of languages.

The Indo-Aryan group, including the tribes of Gujarat, Rajasthan and the Indo-Gangetic Plain converse in languages belonging to this family. Some of the languages belonging to this group include Chhattisgarhi, Gujarati, Marathi, Assamese, Oriya etc.

There is yet another language family spoken by the tribes of the Andaman Islands by tribes such as the Great Andamanese, Onges, Jarawas and the Sentinelese. They speak what is loosely called as the Andamanese language.

Racial Distribution

The racial composition of the tribes of India can be grouped into the following categories:

The Proto-Australoids with dark skin colour, short to medium stature, low forehead, sunken nose, dark complexion and curly hair. The tribes of middle India like the Mundas, the Oraons, the Hos, the Gonds, the Khonds etc. belong to this group.

The Mongoloids with straight hair, flat nose, prominent cheek bones and almond shaped eyes with the epicanthic fold present, yellowish skin colour, medium stature, high head and medium nose. The tribes of north-eastern India and the Himalayan region belong to this category.

The Dravidians include tribes of South India, like the Kadars, the Irulas and the Paniyans.

The Great Andamanese, Onges, Sentinelese and the Siddhis form yet another racial category.

Demographic Size

In India tribal groups vary greatly when we consider their size in terms of total population. On one hand, we find tribal communities like the Gonds, Bhils, with a population of about forty lakhs. The Santhals too have a population size of over thirty lakhs. On the other hand there are more than forty tribes in India which have a population ranging from one to five lakhs. And then, on the extreme end of the spectrum, we have tribal communities like a few Andamanese groups who are even less than hundred in number.

Degree of Assimilation into Mainstream Society

Tribal and non-tribal communities in India have co-existed for centuries, influencing each other in different ways and to varying degrees. The degree of assimilation of the tribal population into non-tribal, caste-based Hindu society varies greatly and tribes have also been classified according to this criterion. The following classifications may be made on this basis.

There are tribal communities who have confined themselves to their original habitats and maintained their distinct traditional pattern of life. Examples of these are the hunting-gathering and hill cultivating tribes of India.

Acculturated tribal communities include those tribal communities who have migrated to urban or semi-urban areas and are engaged in the industrial sector and adopted the cultural traits of the rest of the population, for example, industrial labourers including the Santhal and the Ho.

Totally assimilated tribal communities include those tribes which have been assimilated and are an integral part of the new social order. The Bhumjis, Majhis, Raj Gonds are examples of such assimilated tribal communities.

Mode of Livelihood or Subsistence Pattern

Yet another categorization has been made on the basis of mode or pattern of livelihood. These categories are as follows:

Food Gatherers and Hunters

The economic activities of such tribes include hunting, fishing, gathering and collecting food. Examples of this category include the Chenchu, Challa Yanadi, Malaya Pandaram/Hill Pandaram, Cholanaickan and the Great Andamanese.

Horticulturists

These tribes extract resources from a given area of land and consequently make a greater impact on the environment. The Dongoria Kandha inhabiting Niyamgiri hills of Rayagada district of Odisha are good example of such tribes.

Pastoral tribes have adopted herding as either their primary or secondary source of livelihood. The Bakarwal, Bharwad, Drogpa, Gujjar and Toda are examples of such tribes.

Hill Cultivator Tribes

The people inhabiting the hilly areas have adopted shifting cultivation methods to sustain themselves. This is a slash and burn type of agriculture popularity known as *Podu Chas* in South Odisha. The Adi, Aka, Birjhia, Bondo, Chakma, Chiru, Gangte, Kandha, Jamatia, Juang, Dimasa, Karbi, Miji, Mishmi, Ao, Konyak, Phom, Paite, Riang, Tangsa, Wancho are examples of this category.

Agriculturists

Agriculture is the primary source of livelihood for most of the tribal population of India. Tribal communities, like the Apatani, Chero, Deori, Miri, Ho, Jaintia, Khamba, Kharia, Khasi, Kolam, Tiwa, Rabha, Kinnaura, Bhumij, Santhal, Munda, Oraon, Kharwa, Baiga, Gond, Bhil, Mina, Warli, Koya belong to this category.

Simple Artisans

There are number of tribes in India who subsist on traditional craft traditions and cottage industries, like basketry, wood craft, weaving, iron smelting, rope making etc. Except in few cases, these are usually subsidiary occupations. For example, the Asur, Goduliya Lohar, Agaria are iron smiths; the Birhors are rope makers; the Gara are blacksmiths; the Kota and the Tharua are potters; and the Saunta and the Mahali are basket-makers.

Folk Artists

There are certain tribes in India who are traditional singers, dancers, bards, acrobats and snake-charmers. Some of the tribes belonging to this category are the Nat, Sapera, Kela, Pardhan, Ojha, Pamula, Kalbelia, Mons, Paradhist etc.

Skilled Workers and White Collar Jobs

In the post-Independence era, the Constitution of India has helped in creating job opportunities for tribal people by reserving seats in different services. As a result we find tribal people are employed in offices, hospitals, administrative jobs etc.

STs of Odisha

Odisha occupies a unique position among the States for the highest concentration of Scheduled Tribes numbering 81.45 lakh (40.66 lakh males and 40.78 lakh females) (2001 census). 22.13 per cent of the total population of the state comprised STs. The ST population of the state has gone up to 95.90 lakh with 47.27 lakh males and 48.63 lakh females. The ST population came to 22.84 per cent to the total population of the State. The districts of Koraput, Rayagada, Malkangiri, Nabarangpur, Mayurbhanj, Phulbani and Sundargarh are inhabited by the large number of tribals than other districts of Odisha. The Kandha of Odisha alone is the seventh largest tribal group in India and they are twice the size of the better known Naga people of Assam. In number and group the tribal population is very significant here.

Odisha has as many as 62 varieties of Scheduled Tribes. Territorially, the tribes of Odisha may be broadly divided into three divisions and they are as follows:

(i) Those living in Southern Region of Odisha are the Kandha, Paraja, Gadaba, Gond, Saora, Koya etc.;
(ii) Those living in Northern Region of Odisha are the Munda, Santal, Kolha (Ho), Oraon, Kisan, Bhuiyan etc.; and
(iii) The tribals living in Central Odisha are the Juang and Bhuiyan. Odisha comes under the central tribal belt of the country.

The tribes and natural resources constitute the true cultural and economic strength of Odisha. Tribal villages of Odisha found in different ecological, economic and cultural environments have been differently affected by modern forces of change. These villages are found to have often different types of economic organizations and economic problems, which need to be considered in the light of their cultural characteristics and age-old traditions. In some cases, customs and traditions stand in the way of economic changes. However, with accelerating impact of urbanization and industrialization tribal economic and cultural life are undergoing considerable transformation.

Tribal areas are mostly backward areas of the State. The Scheduled Areas of Odisha fully cover six districts (Mayurbhanj, Sundargarh, Koraput, Rayagada, Nabarangpur and Malkangiri) and seven districts partially (viz., Balasore, Keonjhar, Sambalpur, Kalahandi, Gajapati, Ganjam and Kandhamal). More than 50 per cent of tribal population of the State is found in undivided Koraput district, Mayurbhanj and in Sundargarh districts and 25 per cent of tribal population is found in undivided Koraput districts alone (i.e. present Koraput, Rayagada, Nabarangpur and Malkangiri districts).

In absolute terms the tribal population of the State has increased from 42.24 lakh to 81.45 lakh during 1961-2000. But the percentage of tribal population to total population of the State has declined from 24.07 per cent in 1961 to 22.13 per cent in 2001 Census (However, it was 22.84% in 2011). This may be due to high mortality rate among tribes and also due to low standard of living and difficult environment.

Tribes of Koraput

Koraput district of Odisha is a tribal concentrated district. Tribes of Koraput in general and that of Kuvis (Kandhas) in particular are discussed elaborately in Chapter 3.

SECTION II

Folklore: Meaning and its Components

Folklore is the oral literature of the simpler society. It is perpetuated by oral traditions. Folklore covers almost the entire life experience. It is present in our daily life. It is present in speech such as riddles, jokes; it is present in our games, dance and song. None of these studies of human life, from ethnography, history, linguistics to literature can ignore folklore. Folklore of a tribal community is part of the entire culture of the people. It brings solidarity, continuity, and consistency in a cultural group.

The term "folklore" was established by William Thoms in 1846 and now it is internationally accepted. It is derived from the German word "Volklehre" which means peoples' custom. During nineteenth and twentieth century scholars studied songs, tales and games and defined them as folklore. However, today it includes a wide range of meeting points and comprise a large range of oral and verbal practices as well as material performances including songs, theatre performing art, weaving as well as something like building houses and cooking. Folklore reflects the ancient observances and customs, notions and beliefs, traditions and superstitions and prejudices of the common people. Folklore of the tribes is an important aspect of their culture which is communicated through verbal or expressive literature, behaviour visible through the material life and performances as well as public display.

Definition

In anthropological usage, the term 'folklore' means myths, legends, folk-tales, folk-songs; proverbs, riddles and a variety of forms of artistic expression whose medium is spoken language. It is a part of culture but not the whole culture.

Folklore is conceived variously by different scholars and by several disciplines. It is described as the folk knowledge and wisdom of a group of people. Others term it as an oral tradition. Each society marches ahead; depending upon its folklore. It is medium in which a community expresses itself truly and colourfully. It is a set of cultural connections, which is realistic, artistic and communicative. It stands for the blue print of human actions everywhere.

Folk culture cannot be demarcated through geographical notions or by literary reasons alone. It belongs to people of similar race, gender, religion or occupation. It can cut across geographical boundaries and have close man to man interaction. It can also be shaped by technology and modern society. Folk always implies some kind of collectivity. Folk does not necessarily imply rural or lower class. There can be strong urban literate folk. Television, computers, telephone all have impacted folk genres, such as jokes, songs, stories and myths. It also has become a great tool in transmission and the generation of new folk culture.

Folk culture is alive and vibrant. In the nineteenth century, folklore was considered to be a dead culture. But, it is vibrant ever changing cultural tradition of any region.

Folk culture comprises learned habits, beliefs, rituals, institutions and expressions of the people. This is strictly limited to oral habits and includes material culture as well.

Folklore can be global or local, national or international, personal or public. Folklore also remains deeply authentic and reliable. Continuity of tradition proves to its authenticity.

So, folklore may be defined as a broad category that can be said to be the culture of any group that is communicated through verbal or expressive literature, behaviour visible through the material life (including customs, rituals) and performance and public display of the individual.

Simply we may say that folklore is the oral literature of the simpler societies in general and that of the tribals in particular. They are learnt by the ear, and transmitted from generation to generation.

Genres of Folk Culture

It is generally accepted that folk life embraces the whole panorama of human life and traditional culture that includes traditional art and craft as well as oral culture. The various genres of folk culture may be stated as follows:

Oral Literature

Oral literatures are spoken, sung or merely voiced forms of verbal communications that show some repeated behaviour. This is sometimes defined as verbal or communicative art. These may be:

Oral Narratives/Stories/Tales

Folk narratives encompass all genres of oral literature. The tales provide a sense of fantasy to the listener. The tales can be having factious, historical, revered or ridiculed treatments and plots. The characters may be mortal, divine, supernatural or human. The '*Panchatantra*' stories are very popular folk narratives.

Folk Poetry

In the manner of its transmission folk poetry can be differentiated from narrative. Oral epics come under this group. Poetry is often repetitive, dramatic and exaggerated. This often deals with materials of dramatic local significance. Epics on the other hand are poems that are highly ornamental dealing with the adventures of extraordinary people. They can be heroic, romantic and historic. The *Mahabharata* and the *Ramayana* are two major epics of our country.

Proverbs

These are sort of well-known sayings that speak about general truth or gives advice. They are short, witty traditional expressions that arise as part of our everyday discourse as well as highly structured situations like education. They often take a personal circumstance and embody it in a witty form.

Riddles

Riddles are witty and puzzling questions relating to something abscure, they are framed with the purpose of confusing or testing the wits of those who do not know the answers. Usually, they have confusing descriptions and often describe a scene.

Folk Speech

Folk speech are the everybody spoken common language of the people. These speeches are used on certain special occasions. Such items as teasing, joking, taunting, cursing, blessing, chanting, oath taking, insulting and sarcastically speaking are some of the expressions which come under the folk speech of folklore. Similarly gestures, greetings, bidding farewell, nicknaming etc. are also the folk speech.

This is highly informed way of talking that is learned by linguistic acculturation and by observing language patterns from family, friends and associations.

Important Functions of Folklore

For the tribals, the functions performed by the folklore are important. Different forms of folklore perform different functions. For example the lullaby is used to put the children to sleep. A love song gives enthusiasm to young couples. Old people tell stories to their ancestors and in the process they educate the children. A work song helps the men and women to synchronize their efforts. Folk songs or folk tales incorporating morals are introduced to inculcate diligence and filial piety and to ridicule laziness, rebelliousness and snobbishness. Mostly the formal instructions are given in the youth dormitories. Some of the verbal instructions during the marriage ceremonies of boys and the preparation of girls for marriage are given in the form of songs. The songs of ridicule are important as a means of censuring misbehaviour (Vidyarthi and Rai, 1985: 316).

Material Culture

Material culture refers to the techniques transmitted across generations and all the processes that are hand made and used by men. Some of the important genres are:

Crafts and Art

Any item having artistic or utilitarian functions that is hand made and has been passed down by tradition comes under craft. This is different from art and occupation. It has immense aesthetic appeal and requires workmanship.

Any object that gives some pleasure and also serves some practical social or economic purpose can be called art. It has an aesthetic appeal. This object is popular and is not subject to rapidly changing fashions.

The basic difference between craft and art may be:

> The item in which pleasure giving functions predominate, the artifact is called art, and if a practical function predominates in the item it is called craft. In carving and engraving, clay modelling, painting, weaving, and tattooing etc., we find the examples of graphic and plastic arts.

Folk Architecture

Folk architecture may be said as traditional architecture. It is concerned with all traditional aspects of building, the shapes, sizes and its layout, the material used and the tools and techniques of building; the sites chosen and the placement of various buildings; the use and functionality of such buildings.

Folk Costumes

The dresses of all traditional, ethnic, occupational and sectarian groups come under this category. It is determined geographically and it expresses the region or the locality that comes under this category. It differs from sector to sector and region to region.

Folk Cookery

It is the cookery practice of common men. This can be described as opposite of commercial and institutional cookery. This includes the study of foods themselves, their composition, their preparation, their preservation, social and psychological functions. It has regional variation, variation in attitudes, taboos, food habits etc.

Social Folk Custom

Social folk custom is based on group interactions rather than individual skills and performances. Some of the subgenres include:

Celebrations and Festivals

Almost all communities periodically set aside some time for celebrations. These are moments of special significance to the entire community. They may be seasonal, anniversaries of historical events, birth or death of a hero or of a god or with religious significance. These might be moments in which some living or dead is honoured with feasting and some performances.

Recreation and Games

There are forms of expressive behaviour and can be non-productive in nature. The goals are in-built. The main objective behind the game is recreation and pleasure.

Folk Medicine

This consists of natural or herbal folk medicine. This may also include magical religious folk medicines. In natural or herbal medicine cure is sought from herbs, plants, minerals and animal substances while magical religious medicines attempt at curing through charms, holy words and actions, in other words, occultism.

Folk Religion

These are orally transmitted popular beliefs amongst the people. This recognizes one or more deity, spirits and demons, personal and impersonal power, ghosts, fate, luck and magic. In this relationalism and science make very little impact. They also embrace the attitudes, bahaviours and culture values of the people.

Performing Folk Art

Performing folk arts are conscious presentations by individuals or groups with folk instruments dance, costumes and props. Some of its subgenres are:

Folk Drama

Folk dramas are performances that occur in festivals and rituals. They use conventional symbols such as customs and the performances take place through stylized actions. It is essentially a public performance and local language makes it easy to understand. They often use many techniques such as dancing, singing, bombastic speeches to attract the audiences.

Folk Music

This is all traditional music that is orally transmitted and passed down by ear and performed by memory. It is not written down and also does not have any musical score. The origin of music remains largely unknown.

Folk Dance

A traditional, anonymously choreographed dance that is communally derived can be called folk dance. It has a strong regional or local characteristic. It is usually also expressed vernacularly and is often a product of change and innovation.

Folk Song

Folk songs punctuate their individual and social life. Appropriate to different social and ritual occasions different songs are sung and different dances are performed. Folk songs are part of life of many communities and source of enjoyment and relaxation. Different musical instruments are used in accompaniment of singing and dancing. Folk song or poems are charged with livid intensity. Often passionate experiences speak simply, quietly and without any concern to decorate or beautify their thoughts and feelings. Their theme is universal and timeless.

SECTION III
A Brief Methodological Analysis

The socio-economic ingredients are contained in the cultural heritage of tribes. Folklore is an important aspect of culture of the tribes. Tribal folklore transmits their customs, traditions and conventions through oral lore. So, their entire life styles along with socio-economic aspects are genuinely reflected in their folklore.

So, an in-depth study of folklore can unlash the real and authentic socio-economic practices of the tribes in general and in that of the present study, "Kuvi" (or Kandha) in particular.

Objectives

The present study has been undertaken with the following objectives:

- To study the cultural values of folklore and their socio-economic importance in the life of the Kuvi (Kandha tribe);
- To document and record some of the important folklores, like oral narratives, folk poetry, proverbs, riddles, folk speech, crafts and art, folk architecture, folk customs, folk cookery, celebrations and festivals, performing folk arts etc. of the Kuvi tribe and to find out their socio-economic values containing their social life, life cycle and socio-political institutions. These also include their economic importance relating to agriculture cycles, forests, dongar and other institutions and activities of economic importance;
- To understand how folklore creates a unique cultural identity of the Kuvi; and
- To suggest some viable measures to promote and preserve Kuvi folklore, which possesses immense socio-economic importance and enrich their overall culture at large.

Hypotheses

The present study is based on the following hypotheses which need to be tested:

- Folklore of the Kuvi tribe is an important element of their culture and plays an indispensable role in their socio-economic life.

- Folklore of the Kuvi is gradually loosing its significance due to the influence of the so called modern civilization.
- Folklore of the Kuvi tribe contains in them high human values and have socio-economic importance.
- The human values and social integrity contained in their folklore are still of educational importance not only for the concerned tribe but for the humanity at large.

Methodology

Both secondary and primary sources of information are taken into account in order to carry out the study. Primary sources of information include personal interview with the people, participatory and not participatory observation, case studies and focus group discussions. Secondary sources include, published books, articles and research papers and reports on the tribal folklore in general and that of the Kuvi in particular.

The Universe and Sample

In the present study areas of Kuvi concentration in Koraput district of Odisha is taken as the universe and Laxmipur block is purposefully selected as sample. Laxmipur block is one among the four major Kuvi concentrated blocks (other three blocks are Narayanpatna, Bandhugaon and Pottangi) of Koraput district. The percentage of the Kuvi population to the total tribal population of Laxmipur block is nearly 90 per cent. Care will be taken to see that the sampling will be done in such a manner that folklore of Kuvis shall be appropriately analysed to reach a meaningful conclusion.

Procedure of Information Collection

The scholar had several visits to the randomly selected villages in order to collect required information on folklores. Efforts were made to find out the socio-economic values contained in such folklore. Though folklore is commonly used by most of the Kuvi, but there are some experts in their communities who may be regarded as treasure house of folklore. The scholar has identified them and collected required information through their songs, riddles, myths, stories and other performances, Interviews, focus group discussion, questionnaire, observation and using secondary data from books, journals, periodicals etc. were the major tools of data collection.

Analysis of Data

Data or information so collected from primary and secondary sources were analysed and scrutinized. Folk tales, myths, legends, folk songs, riddles, proverbs, folk speeches and stories having socio-economic importance were recorded and analysed.

Limitations

Folklore is the mirror of the tribal culture. It is the treasure house of their socio-cultural life. So, it was difficult on the part of the scholar to cover all types of folk traditions and folklores. Though tribal folk-culture covers both material and non-material aspects of their culture, the present study is limited to non-material aspects relating to songs, tales, stories, myths, riddles etc. The area of study is limited to Laxmipur block of Koraput district. However, efforts have been made to see that the sample in the study adequately represent the universe on the Kuvi folklore. As mentioned above the main aim of the study is to find out the socio-economic importance of tribal folklore in general and that of the Kuvis (Kandhas) in particular. Special care has been taken to explore the human values contained in such folklores.

2

TRIBAL CULTURE AND TRIBAL FOLKLORE — AN ANALYSIS

In this chapter an attempt has been made to look into the concept of culture in general and that of tribal culture in particular. An humble attempt has also been made to differentiate tribal folklore and tribal culture in general.

Before going to discuss about tribal culture, it is felt necessary to define 'culture' and state its characteristics as well as its types.

Meaning of Culture

There are various definitions of culture offered by sociologists, philosophers, cultural historians, anthropologists etc. They all try to encapsulate the different aspects of culture. Culture is something that is not transmitted though our genes, but through symbols that are learned in the process of socialization. All culture is learned, but not everything learned is culture. Different communities or societies have different sets of values. Sometimes, these differences may lead to conflicts. The symbols of culture themselves do not mean anything unless they are interpreted with significance by human beings. It is also possible for a sub-culture to exist within a community. Politics, economics, ethics, religion etc. are all factors that influence and are in turn, influenced by culture.

The Oxford Dictionary states the meaning of culture as "customs and civilization of a particular time or people and intellectual and artistic achievement or expression."

Culture also signifies "*Sanskriti*" originating from "*Sanskara*" which is imbued with the sense of a process of enhancement and cleansing. "*Sanskriti*" could then be taken to mean a collection of techniques or a system that purifies and elevates man's existence by showing him how to co-exist in harmony with others and teaches him the ways of living in human society and the practice of philanthropy. It also gathers ambit; those values and modes of conduct which bring about refinement and instills those *Sanskara*, which will take them to enlightenment which will refine their talents.

Prof. Edward Burnett Tylor (1874) said "Culture is a multifaceted set of belief, art, law, morals, customs and any other capabilities and habits acquired by a man as a member of society."

Describing culture as both the result and foundation of instruction, Pandit Jawaharlal Nehru declared that it was fundamental for the creation and growth of both physical and mental attributes.

Roop Rekha Verma defined culture in her book "*Culture and Modernity*" that it is a system of the patterns and the modes of expectations, expressions, values, institutionalization and enjoyment habits of people in general."

Sri Rajgopalacharya said that "culture was the collective expression of the thoughts, speeches and deeds of the learned, talented or creative members of a society or a nation."

Hence, it is difficult to give one universal definition that would cover all aspects of culture because both the meaning and aim of culture are so vast. In culture can be found, the origin and evolution of all the thoughts, customs, objectives and ethics of a particular country or society. Culture is static yet dynamic as it persists and keeps expanding and developing. It is the foundation of the lifestyle of a nation and it continuously supports the progress of the members of the society towards a civilized, liberal and enlightened way of life. It is collection of abstract concepts that have gradually evolved from time immemorial which have contributed to the growth of human society. For any nation, its cultural values form the basis of its progress and its power which can thus, without exaggeration, be called the real wealth of a nation.

In brief, the culture, in ordinary parlance may be defined as the sum total of a nations or society's thinking and living. It is the way of life based on common traditions and environment. It is the common learned way of life shared by members of a society. It implies the behaviour of the people, their ethos, views and value system.

Material and Non-material Culture

Culture has two aspects, i.e. material and non-material. Material aspects of the culture are the science, technology, clothing and food habits etc.

The non-material aspects of culture are the values, goals, world views, thought systems, languages and symbol, status, role system etc. Hence, the belief, ideas and attitudes, religious, social, political and economic organizations, science and technology are all parts of the complex network that is called culture.

The Characteristics of Culture

William Haviland has identified four basic characteristics of culture. They are as follows:

- First, culture is that it is common to a group of people who make up a particular society. Culture is like an ensemble of singers that every persons puts up for the others so that he/she can be identified in a distinct manner;
- Second, it is not hereditary but something that is learned after birth during the period of socialization. Culture is the different ways of knowing not only others but also ourselves;
- Third, culture is associated with various symbols such as an image, an object of worship, rituals, texts and artifacts to continue its flow and it is dependent on people following the codes of conventions associated with a specific culture; and
- Fourth, culture is an amalgamation of social, economic and political features. Culture as a whole is the way of life or a structure of feeling.

Some of the other important characteristics of culture may be stated as follows:

- It is the backbone of any society, whether it is the art, traditions, festivals, ceremonies, even dress and food. If, for any reason there is any block or interference in the growth and transmission of cultural values, the entire structure of that particular society would change.
- Culture may be regarded as the reflection of a spiritual force that precedes all thoughts and interactions.
- Culture differs according to place, time, community and race and this is natural, whenever a particular culture is founded upon values of universal significance, it expands and lasts even after the society that gave rise to it is wiped out.
- If a culture is too rigid, does not adapt, or is not dynamic, then it would be lost. Culture is like a stream or river that flows

around obstacles, changing course when needed without stopping its flow. Hence, culture is not a static thing, it is dynamic one and it also changes.

So, everyone's life is influenced by culture that surrounds him. If we were to distance ourselves from our culture, our lives would cease to have a direction and flow and it is, therefore, essential for us to maintain vibrant contact with our cultural heritage.

Types of Culture

Culture may be broadly divided into the following types: (1) High culture, (2) Low culture, (3) Popular culture, and (4) Folk culture.

High Culture

It may be defined as "taste", under which can be found etiquette, appreciation of better food and wine etc. It also refers to certain social rules that are meant for the upper class and which are not accessible to the lower classes.

The term "high culture" was introduced in English by the Victorian Poet-critic Matthew Arnold through his work "*Culture and Anarchy*" (1869). For him "High Culture" was a force that encouraged moral and political good. He said that this meant to "know the best that has been said and thought in the world" and he defined high culture as the "study of perfection".

Much of "high culture" pertains to the appreciation of "high culture", a term that includes literature, performing arts, music and the visual arts. It also refers to paintings or cinema by the acknowledged masters, classical music or dance and writings that has been established as canons.

Governments of various countries also promote it by funding museums and libraries and subsidizing theatre or music groups.

Low Culture

This is a disparaging term, used for some varieties of popular culture and viewed as opposite to 'high culture'. In the post-modern era, it often appears that the line of distinction between both has almost been erased. And some theorists opine that 'high' and 'low' cultures are subcultures.

Low culture is also another term for popular culture, i.e. that which has mass appeal. This could include things in society as diverse as gossip magazines or talk shows, sports like cricket, commercial films etc.

Popular Culture

In fifteenth century the word 'popular' when used in law and politics, denoted 'low', 'base', 'vulgar' and of the common people. It is in the eighteenth century that the word gained positive connotation and its meaning today is 'widespread' and 'well-linked'.

This type of culture is also known as Pop culture and it is related to all those activities that are popular or common. Popular culture is also taken to mean all those cultural factors that are widely prevalent in particular society and which are transmitted through the local language.

Popular culture features constant change and is limited by both space and time. It is also often defined as mass culture which is commercially driven, mass-produced and is meant for mass consumption. It can also be termed as the 'authentic' culture because it mostly reflects the tastes and fashions of the majority of that period. Popular culture has been seen to have emerged from the shift to urbanization after the industrial revolution.

However, some works appear to blur the fine line that demarcate "high" and "popular" culture and seem to belong to both categories for one or the other reasons.

Folk Culture

This is the tradition and customs of a particular community or society that is reflected in the local life style. Folk culture is usually transmitted from generation to generation through the oral tradition and is imbued with a strong feeling of community. During the pre-industrial era, folk-culture was equivalent to mass culture and hence could also be called the popular culture of that time.

Folklore was and is a part of popular culture that is usually spread through the word of mouth and is transmitted through ear.

Folk culture is firmly rooted to a sense of place, even when some elements of it are shifted to a new locate, as in the case of migration, the displaced elements still carry strong connotations of the place of their origin. That is what distinguishes folk culture from popular culture. However, folk culture has influenced both "Popular" and "High" culture and many features of folk culture have gone on to become an indistinguishable and inextricable part of both these cultures.

Tribal Folklore and Folk Culture

Folklore of tribal people is an integral part of the folk culture. The simple cultural experiences of the tribal people as well as their rich traditions of living in the lap of nature find collective and spontaneous expression in their folk-songs, folk-tales, riddles, proverbs and other oral narratives.

Folklore being a reflector of entire tribal culture brings solidarity, continuity and consistency in cultural group. A sacred tribal tale, for example, may tell the justification of rituals or to illuminate religious mysteries, is of the greatest importance in that it systematizes belief and regulates conduct. Again a legand; or incident in tribal history may also contribute to the building up morals.

Folklore is the oral literature of the simple societies and is perpetuated by oral traditions. Usually, there is no technique of teaching, certainly no formal technique, connected with the making and singing of songs; they are learnt by the ear, and transmitted in this fashion from generation to generation. There is neither conscious awareness of forms or construction on the part of the folk-singer or folk-teller nor there is any aesthetic or analytical theory in his mind.

Functions of Tribal Folklore

Folklore belongs to all; it contains the whole gamut of the society. For the tribal people the functions of folklore are more important than its form. Also they care little about its origin or definition. The lullaby is for putting children to sleep, while love-song gives enthusiasm to young couples. The old feel elevated by telling stories of their ancestors and tries to educate their younger generation and so on.

There are diverse functions of folklore. Some of the most common functions include aiding in the education of young, promoting a group feeling of solidarity, providing socially sanctioned ways for individual's act or to censure other individuals serving as a vehicle for social protest, offering an enjoyable escape from reality and converting dull work into play.

Different types of folklore can share similar, if not identical, functions. In a verbal dwelling situation, one can use tales, riddles and proverbs. Among other kinds of folklore, the function is same though the form is different. Also, any one item of folklore may have diverse functions. A work-song which may synchronize their efforts may also be sung by children for entertainment. Here the form is same; the function is different.

Some of the major areas that folklore fulfils certain functional roles. These are as follows:

Psychological or Individual Functions

Folklore among the tribal people is largely personal and is shaped through people's behaviours, motivations and habits. By and large, folklore is entertaining; it thus gives amusement to the community members. Jokes, riddles, metaphors, tales and performances as well as the arts are the types of folklore that highly entertain the tribes.

Archetypes and heroic figures instill courage and love amongst the listeners. Folk customs, rituals and narratives enrich individual interaction with the community. Stories and anecdotes assert often cultural symbols and values and shapes individuality.

Folklore among the tribal people maintains group cohesion and interaction. For example, children's games, further bond the child not only to his mother, but also with the entire community.

Superstitions, games and riddles often reflect the social context. Individual and social taboos are also either reinforced or denigrated by the folklore.

Myths and legends either mirror or distort the reality of the society and reflect the individual's position in the tribal society.

Functional Aspects

This aspect has been mentioned in the previous section. Folklore gratifies or expresses the hostilities in the culture and society. Proverbs can help to solve legal decisions, while riddles sharpen wit and humour and reinforce cultural values; myths validate conduct in the society, satirical songs release pent up feelings, emotions and tensions. The lullaby is for putting children to sleep, while the love song gives enthusiasm to young couples. The old feels elevated by telling stories of their ancestors. In the process, they try to educate their younger generation.

Above all, folklores help the individual to remain as a cultured member in the society. Some tales about nature also talk about how to grow crops and folk medicines helps to cure diseases. Some customs are purely social and can be described as rites of passage. They help the individual to come closer to society.

Important symbols and values of the people are often expressed in traditions and customs and are passed down from one generation to another. Folklore, hence, passes on pre-existing ethics and standards of the society. This gets also reinforced through performances.

Religious Functions

Religion is a significant part of the daily existence of life. This is expressed in everyday belief, speech, story, performances and song. It also affects both the private practices and public ritual activities and also the material life like clothing, food and objects. Legends about saints like that of sant Kabir and Tukaram, supernatural narratives like the myths of Bhima, Ravan etc. are parts of religious scripts. Magic and occult practices all are deeply religious in content.

Folk religion differs from formal state of religion. Religious motifs, integrate the individual's ideas and practices into a smooth transaction into human society. The belief system is largely communicative.

Some rites are observed periodically. Some other rites are treated as the rites of passage that are associated with human life cycle rituals, such as birth, puberty, marriage, old age and death.

Rituals are important constituents of religion and are often psychologically determined. It also has hidden social goals that make ritual symbolic. Rituals play an important role in transmitting cultural knowledge and religious symbols and it maintains the continuation of the society from past to the present.

Historical and National Functions

Folklore is a strong cultural symbol that advocates national and ethnic pride. This is primarily done through the development, preservation, imitation and collection of literature, language and traditions. The ideas of a strong historical and cultural nationalism arose in the eighteenth and nineteenth century. This greatly emphasized the ideas of the individual and creativity and also it inspired an interest in antiquity, tradition and folklore.

Creation of national language, formation of myths and symbols, such as flags, national anthems and national festivals are influenced by the folklore of the respective countries. Nationalism created through the study of folklore varies according to different socio-cultural and political contexts of different nations.

A deep interest in folklore studies created a cultural consciousness or a cultural movement. Bal Gangadhar Tilak, a famous freedom fighter of India, revived the *Ganesh* festival to arouse nationalistic sentiment among the Maharashtrians. Folklore is used in music, art, dance, drama and literature of different communities.

Economic Functions

Folklore has also made great contributions to the economic life style of the people. This can be seen in the creation of material culture that has economic as well as utilitarian skills. Crafts are one such example. Crafts can be essential to the daily utilities of life as well have some decorative and spiritual functions. So, it has both utilitarian and aesthetic characteristics. Economic activities and pursuits are found place in the folklore of the communities.

Many scholars today feel that crafting is the process of doing rather than creating. In additions to historical crafts through construction of mills, buildings, houses etc. should be seen as processes of crafts. Folklore is also represented in the form of opportunities for consumption and for selling. Indigenous tools, equipments, arts and crafts as well as songs, dances, dramas, dresses and ornaments are great attractions to the folklorists. These, in a planned manner, can be marketed. In this process these will positively contribute to economic growth of a particular area.

Cross-Cultural Functions

All folklore material is based on commonalty and intercultural diffusions. It can create a cultural co-operation amongst nations. Myths seem to originate in ancient sacrificial fertility rituals with the passage of time the myths went their separate ways and rites became customs. Every society lives in pluralistic, open ended and free world in which it possesses its own unique history and values.

So, the important functions of folklore of the tribes are that they educate, validate culture, justify its rituals and institutions to those who perform and observe them. It maintains conformity to the accepted pattern of behaviour. Sometimes folklore permits actions that are usually not approved. There are in very culture words that should not be spoken and deeds that should not be done. However, when such words and deeds appear in the folklore of these communities, they are not taken seriously.

Radicals of Folklore of the Tribes

Some of the radicals of tribal folklore may be mentioned as follows:

1. The first and foremost redial is the mythical tales relating to stories and explanations about the origin of the world, stars etc. They have a number of legends which give their simple, but at the same time fantastic ideas about their traditional history, about the history of man and the ways of woman, about the creation of world, sky, earth, sun, moon, water, thunder and lighting.

   Radicals in Tribal myths can be classified as those dealing with:

   - Periodic, natural and seasonal changes like; regular alteration of day and night, and of winter and summer. The sun and the moon are regarded as beings. The moon and its phases are commonly believed to have an intimate connection with the birth and growth of animals and plants, the sun being male and moon female.
   - Stories relating to extraordinary natural phenomenon explain their origin and cause, and reveal the strong sense of beauty ingrained in the tribes, and their love of colour and flowers. The showers and the rainbow, the lightning and the thunder, the trees and the forest delight them immensely.
   - The tales of the origin or creation of the world, prevalent among a few Indian tribes, reveal "a sweep of imagination and grandeur of conception worthy of epic poets". Myths are related to the origin of animals and mankind etc.
   - The tribal people belief their descent from a common ancestor and their traditional relationships are embedded in elaborate genealogies. Such tribal heroes are believed to be capable of performing many things beyond the powers of man.
   - The tribes have a strong believe in their dead ancestors. The dead were often thought of as having considerable power either for good or evil and are, therefore, objects of worship. The ancestors generally believed to return and help them at the time of pain and stress.

2. The second radical in their folklore is the impact of supernatural being or presence of supernatural elements and they can be of any shape like, a cat, rat, fish, snake or inanimate also.
3. The morals are often underlined in the folklore.
4. Cumulative songs form (another) important element in the folklore.
5. For the sake of rhythm, the rhythms sometimes contain meaningless words and verbal expressions. This is also found in *mantras*, sorcery and witch craft.
6. Folk-songs are recited on religious and social occasions and are much appreciated.
7. The festive occasions always bear some types of story. Whatever may be the type of festivals, they are connected with an ancestor-story.

The tribal folk-tales are very simple in nature and cover a wide range of subjects as evident from the radicals of the folklore.

The folk-song of the tribal people with respect to its verse aspect is again of diverse types and nature. It is not sophisticated. It reflects the joys and sorrows, problems and worries of the common people. Structurally, the tribal folk-songs are very short but its words are repeated during singing to prolong it. Sometimes, a song of a few lines is sung hours together by the singers.

The riddle combines recreational and educational features to an unusual degree. Young people love it for amusement and old people encourage their use because of their instructive value. Further, riddles are socially very significant and, therefore, taboos are associated with their use and sometimes contain references to historical events.

Posing of riddles is not restricted to any particular time of the year. Generally, the evening hours are considered suitable for riddles and telling folk-tales. There is a common belief that the person who tells folk-tales during the day is a fool or time killer. Riddles are played by the young and old as an indoor game in the winter and occasionally as an outdoor game when the weather is fine.

Such are the functions of radicals of folklore in the indigenous societies, that is, the tribes. These folk cultures have enriched the tribal societies since time in immemorial. They are the treasure houses of their value system, their origin and history and cultural continuity. These are also the mirrors of their socio-cultural and socio-economic life.

3

A PROFILE OF KORAPUT DISTRICT AND SOCIO-ECONOMIC LIFE OF THE KUVI (KANDHA)

The Kuvi tribe, as stated earlier, is referred to as the "Kandha" in the Census. But the scholar in his field study found that these people introduce themselves as the Kuvi. Although administration identify them as the "Kandha" but they feel proud to be called as the "Kuvi". So the scholar used the term "Kuvi" instead of "Kandha" in this piece of work.

Koraput — A Brief Historical Background

Koraput region, a part of Dandakaranya, as described in the holy epic *Ramayana* has a hoary past and rich cultural heritage. History records that this area was known as "Trikalinga" which formed parts of the empires of Satavahanas, Vikatakas, Nalas, Marathas, Eastern Gangas, Chalukyas, Somavamsis, Gangas, Kalachuris, Chindikanagas, Matsya dynasty, Silavamsis and lastly the Surya Vanshi (solar dynasty). As many as 25 rules belonging to the Solar race ruled over Jeypore estate (undivided Koraput district) from 1443 A.D. to 28.12.1952. Then the estate was vested in the State Odisha under the provisions of the Orissa Estates Abolition Act, 29.12.1952. Ten "Anchals" were formed for managing the affairs of the estate and regular Ryotwari system of administration was introduced with effect from 14.11.1957.

The then second largest district of the country, i.e. Koraput, was divided into four districts, i.e. Koraput, Rayagada, Nabarangpur and Malkangiri in 1992 for administrative convenience. Koraput region (undivided Koraput district) has a large tribal concentration. Nearly 54 per cent of its inhabitants are the tribes. Here in our analysis Koraput District refers to the divided Koraput District.

A Brief Profile of Koraput District

Location and Boundary

The district is located between 18°13' to 19°10' North latitude and 82°05' to 83°23' East longitude in the southern part of Odisha. Total geographical area of the districts is 8807 sq.km. which covers 5.66 per cent of the total geographical area of state. It is extended in the west up to Bastar district of Chhattisgarh state and Malkangiri district, in the east up to Rayagada District of Odisha and Srikakulam District of Andhra Pradesh, in the south up to Vizayanagrarm and Vishakhapatnam Districts of Andhra Pradesh and in the north up to Nabarangpur and Rayagada districts of Odisha.

Location of Koraput district in Odisha and Map of Koraput district is given in Map 3.1 and Map 3.2.

Physiography

The district is located on a section of the Eastern Ghats in two agro-climatic zones, namely the Eastern Ghat high land (entire Koraput sub-division and Kotpad block) and South-eastern Ghat zone (Jeypore, Borigumma, Kundura and Boipariguda blocks). The district has an

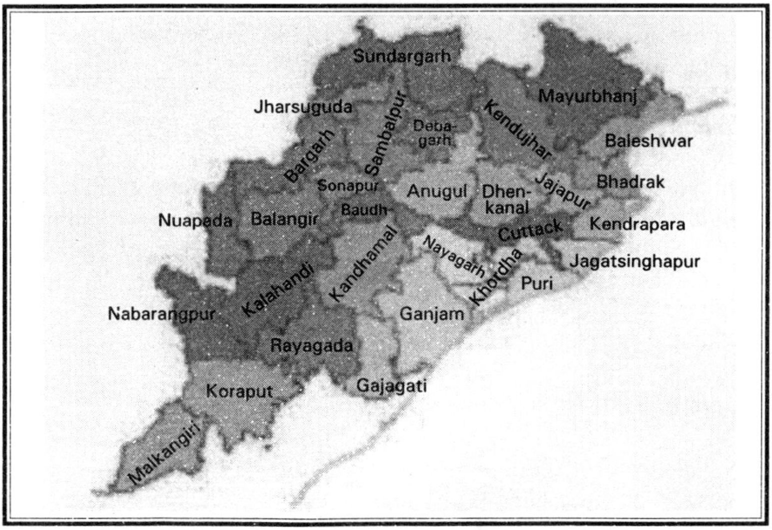

Map 3.1: Map of Odisha

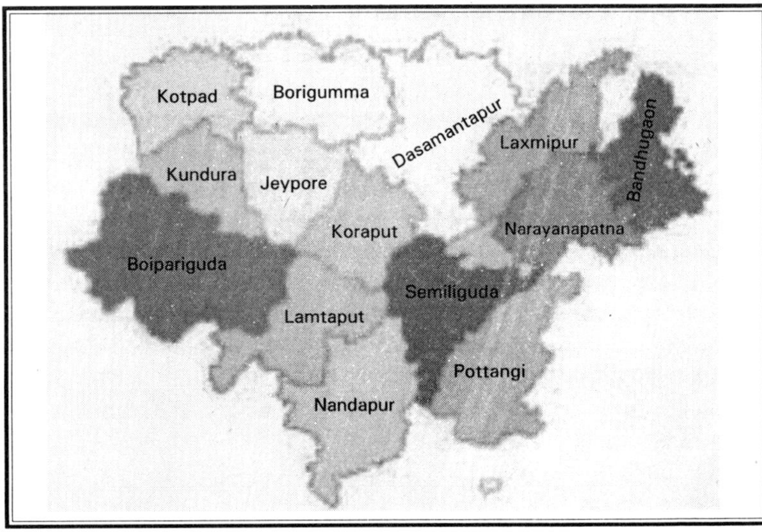

Map 3.2: Map of Koraput District Blocks

altitude ranging between 300 metres and 1000 metres above MSL. The blocks, namely Koraput, Semiliguda, Pottangi, Nandapur, Lamtaput, Dasamantapur and Laxmipur are having altitude over 900 metres above MSL. Narayanapatna and Bandhugaon blocks have altitude ranging between 300 metre and 600 metre above MSL. Jeypore subdivision has altitude up to 600 metre above MSL.

Climate

The climate is warm and humid with mean summer maximum temperature of 34.1°C during the summer and in winter minimum temperature of 7.5°C. During winter, in high altitude area of Semiliguda and Pottangi, the temperature goes down from 2°C to 3°C. To sum up, the monsoon is wet and humid; the winter is cool and prolonged, and the summer is mild and pleasant.

Rainfall

The district is affected by depressions from Bay of Bengal. It causes widespread heavy rainfall and high wind. The average rainfall of the district is 1521.8 mm. 80 per cent of the rainfall is received during June to September. The district actually received rain during 2000 and 2001 was 1398.7 mm and 1528.9 mm respectively. In 2011 Kotpad block received the highest amount of 1867.3 mm and Pattangi block the lowest amount of 349.1 mm rainfall. (*Source: District Statistical Hand Book*, 2011).

Predominant Economic Activities

Agriculture is the mainstay of the economy of the district. Traditionally, people take up agriculture along with animal husbandry, collection of minor forest produces, petty business and transport operations. Of late farmers have switched over to vegetables, spices, sugarcane and maize cultivations.

Major Food/Commercial Crops and Plantation/Horticulture Crops

Coffee and cashew are emerging as major commercial plantation crops. Along with coffee plantation, other activities like sericulture, oil palm, mango, guava, citrus, banana, commercial vegetables, spices like ginger/ turmeric etc. are also being taken up on moderate scale. In addition to these, there is good potential for medicinal and aromatic crops, spawn production unit, cattle breeding farms, organic vegetable production and coffee processing in the district (Potential linked credit plan 2009-10 NABARD, Orissa Regional Office, BBSR). Paddy, *raggi*, and other minor millets are the food crops which are traditionally grown in the district.

Land Utilization Pattern

The district has a forest area of 1879.53 sq.km. The net area sown, otherwise called as cultivated area amounts to be at 2,40,897 hectares. The area with miscellaneous trees and groves not included in net area sown is 20,900 hectares, permanent pasture and other grazing land 16,149 hectares, cultivable waste land 12,078 hectares, land put to non-agriculture uses 32,211 hectares barren and uncultivable lands 1,14,932 hectares, current fallows 74,114 hectare and other fallows 18,382 hectares (*District Statistical Handbook*, Koraput, 2001).

Major Crops and Agricultural Productivity

Paddy is the major crop of the district. *Raggi* is the second major crop from the non-paddy section, which constitutes an important food item of rural households. The total area under paddy cultivation is 1,52,442 hectares (2000-01) having the production of 34,50,385 qtls. with a yield rate of 22.63 qtls. per hectare. The yield rate of paddy had been increased to 27.06 qtls./hect. during 2003-04 (*Economic Survey*, Odisha, 2004-05).

The coverage of *Raggi* in the District is 37,598 ha having production of 2,05,515 qtls. with the yield rate of 5.47 qtls./ha. The other crops include wheat, maize, green gram, black gram, horse gram, niger, groundnut, mustard, potato, sugarcane etc.

The overall agricultural productivity per worker is 4.68 qtls./year. The average size of tilling per cultivator is 1.62 qtls./hect., i.e. 4 acres (2000-01).

Major Tribes of Koraput Region

The major tribes with population more than one lakh are the Kuvi in Koraput and Rayagada, Paraja of Koraput, Koya of Malkangiri and Bhottadas and Gonds of Nabarangpur. The tribes with population more than 50,000 and less than one lakh are the Bhottada and Gadaba of Koraput, Bhumia of Malkangiri, Paraja of Nabarangpur and Saora of Rayagada district. On the other hand, the Bhumia of Koraput, Paraja of Malkangiri, Kuvi of Nabarangpur and Sabara of Rayagada have a population more than 20,000 and less than 50,000 each. Tribal population with various ranges is presented in Table 3.1. There are about 54 numbers of tribes both big and small from numerical point of view in Koraput district. Similarly, there are 56 categories of tribes in Malkangiri, 53 categories in Nabarangpur, 45 categories in Rayagada district of the region. The tribes live under varying ecological situations and their economy is conditioned accordingly.

The Kuvi Tribe: A Socio-Economic Profile

The "Kuvi" (or the "Kondhs", as they are identified by administration), are the largest tribal group in Odisha, numbering over one million. Out of 68 varieties of tribes numerically the "Kondh" is the largest group in Koraput (undivided) region by their population.

The Kuvi have racial affinity with Proto-Australoid stock with Mongoloid admixture. They have dark brown to neatly black skin, medium structure and broad nose and broad head. The Kuvi are Dravidian people but no mythology or legend yet discovered to furnish any clue to their origin or place of descent.

Table 3.1: Tribes with Various Range of Population

Sl. No.	*Range of ST Population*	*Districts with Name of Tribes*			
		Koraput	*Malkangiri*	*Nabarangpur*	*Rayagada*
1.	1 lakh and more	Kuvi, Paraja	Koya	Bhottada, Gond	Kuvi
2.	50,000 & more but less than 1 lakh	Bhottada, Gadaba	Bhumia	Paroja	Saora
3.	20,000 & more but less than 50,000	Bhumia	Paroja	Kuvi	Shabar
4.	10,000 & more but less than 20,000	Kondadora, Omanatya, Parenga	Gadaba, Kuvi	—	Paraja, Jatapu
5.	5000 & more but less than 10,000	Kotia, Pentia	Bondo, Dharua, Didayi, Kondadora, Kotia	Omanatya, Saora	—
6.	1000 & more but less than 5000	Bhumij, Holva, Kuvia, Gouda, Santal, Saora	Bhuiya,Bhumij, Hoiva, Kuvi Gouda, Matya Santal	Banjara, Bhunjia, Gadaba, Holva, Kuvi Gouda, Munda, Santal, Shabar	Kondadora
7.	500 & more but less than 1000	Bhuiya, Dharua, Matya, Oraon, Shabar	Banjara, Gandia, Parenga, Saora, Shabar	Bhumia, Dharua, Kondadora	Gadaba, Kuvi Gouda, Kolha Loharas, Munda
8.	100 & more but less than 500	Pathudi, Bondo, Ganda, Kawar, Kharia, Kissan, Kolha, Madia, Mahali, Munda	Bothoda, Gond, Kora, Munda, Oraon, Kisan, Kolha	Bagata, Bhuiya, Bonda, Gandia, Kolha Loharas, Lodha, Mahali Oraon, Sounti	Kharia, Koya, Matya, Santal
9.	Less than 100	Bagata, Baiga, Banjara, Bhuiya, Binjhal, Dal, Didayi, Gandia, Ghara, Ho, Jatapu, Juang, Khawar, KoI, Kolha Loharas, Koli, Kora, Korua, Koya, Kulis, Lodha, Mundari, Sounti, Tharua	Bagata, Baiga, Bathudi, Bhunjia, Binjhal, Binjhia, Chenchu, Desua Bhumij, Ghara, Ho, Jatapu, Juang, Kawar, Kharia, Kol, Kolha Loharas, Koli, Korua, Kulis, Lodha, Madia, Mahali, Mirdha, Omanatya, Pentia, Rajaur, Sounti, Tharua	Balhudi, Bhumij, Binjhar, Birhor, Desua, Ho, Jatapu, Juang, Kawar, Kharia, Kharwar, Kisan, KoI, Kolha, Koli, Kora, Korua, Kotia, Koya, Kulis, Madia, Mankidi, Mirdhas, Mundari, Parenga, Pentia, Rajuar, Saunti, Tharua	Bagata, Bonjara, Bhottoda, Bhuiya, Bhumia, Bhumij, Bhunjia, Binjhal, Binjhia, Bondo, Dharua, Didayi, Gandia, Gond, Ho, Kawar, Kol, Kolha, Kora, Kotia, Kulis, Lodha, Madia, Mirdha, Mundari,Omanatya, Oraon, Sounti, Tharua

Source: Compiled by Dr. J. Samal basing on 2001 Census Reports.

Recent studies of some of the scholars indicate that the roots of a number of "Kuvi" words are closer to Tamil than to Telugu, despite the much greater distance between the two language areas. They may throw interesting lights on the pre-history of both of them who claim that the Kuvi are a pre-Dravidian people.

However, variations in belief and cultural practices between the sub-groups make it far more likely that the one and a half-million Kuvi speaking people have grown together from groups on the plains who retreated first from Dravidian and then from Aryan invaders at different time since 4000 B.C.

Economic Life

The Kuvi, however, born and bred in the midst of rugged hills, dense forests, deep water courses and insalubrious climate, experienced an economic life that was radically different from that of the people of the plains. The economic life of the Kuvi and their survival is based on agriculture and forest. Agriculture is the chief occupation of the tribal people of Odisha. Most of the Kuvi claimed to be the original owners of the soil. Referring to the Kuvi (Kandhas) H.H. Risley writes "they claim full rights of property in the soil by virtue of having cleaned the jungle and prepared the land for cultivation. In some villages individual ownership is unknown and the land is cultivated on a system of temporary occupation subject to periodical redistribution under the orders of the headman." They are mostly shifting cultivators in South Odisha, i.e. Koraput region. Shifting cultivation, foods gathering, forest collection, and to some extent wage labour regulate their economic life.

Agriculture

The Kuvi practise both Shifting and Settled cultivation. Shifting Cultivation is known as "*Horu tasa*" by the Kuvi, but it is popularly known as "*Podu chasa*" in Koraput region. In such cultivation plots are either clan owned or privately owned. The plots are distributed by the headman of each village in consultation with the village elders. During summer, they clean the forest and burn it. After felling trees, branches and leaves dried, in the ashes thus available, they sow seed with the commencement of the rains. After raising one or two crops, the Kuvis allowed it to remain fallow for few years. In the mean time, the trees grew sufficiently to allow a second felling. Then the same process is continued until the land shows signs of exhaustion. They then finally abandon this land and they clear a fresh jungle for future crops. Shifting cultivation (*Podu*) is carried on the hills and hill slopes.

However, it is a rain-fed type of agriculture with primitive, crude and unscientific methods of cultivation. The production of land both per acre and per worker is quite low. Availability of plain and flat lands for settled agriculture is quite limited. Good quality of settled land has been alienated since long from them by others due to various socio-economic reasons. Still the plain land agriculture of the Kuvi, where it is practised, suffers from uneconomic holding, tenure disincentive, crude technology, low investment etc.

Forest Collection

The Kuvis collect forest produce to supplement their income from agriculture. They collect minor forest produce, house building materials, fuel wood, herbal medicines etc. from the forest. They also go for hunting during their leisure time. But, scope of hunting is now quite limited due to large scale deforestation and restrictions imposed on it. They collect various types of fruits, roots, tubers, leaves and fibres to supplement their food requirements. Tribe's life mainly clusters around the forests. Economically, ecologically, socially and culturally tribal life is inseparable from forest. The agriculture of the Kuvi is to a great extent on forest based. The return from agriculture being quite low and unrewarding, the forest resources fast degrading, the economic life of the Kuvis of Koraput region in general and that of the Laxmipur block in particular is becoming less lucrative day by day.

Live Stock

The Kuvis rear cows, buffaloes, goats, pigs and fowls. The cattle are also used for ploughing. Other animals are sold for cash or required for sacrifice in socio-religious activities. The Kuvi generally do not milch their cows. Animal husbandry is not a commercial enterprise for the Kuvi.

Wage Work

Wage earning now-a-days becomes another source of major income of the Kuvi. The Kuvi also work for their own people at a very low wage rate or in exchange for some food and drink. Exchange and cooperative labour have been usual practice among them prevailing since long.

Trade and Commerce

The Kuvi generally are not interested in trade and commerce. On the contrary, they detested trade and considered it a degrading occupation. Trade and commerce in the Kuvi areas are mostly done by the communities, such as the S.C., Dom, Sundhi (Wine Venders), Kumuti money lenders and traders, and some outside Odia persons.

Cottage Craft

The Kuvis also practise Cottage crafts, like rope making, leaf plate making, weaving, spinning, knitting, blacksmithy, stone carving, wood work, bamboo basket making etc. Such practices depend upon the availability of local resources and skills as well as markets.

The Social Life

Most of the Kuvi habitations are of small units consisting of 5 to 100 houses. These are scattered too. The village site is usually selected with reference to the geographical situation which is not frequented by the Carnivorous animals, proximity of the village to a source of water and close availability of agricultural fields.

Housing

The traditional houses of the Kuvi are mud houses with "*Piri*" (straw) thatched. Now-a-days gradually the houses are either built or renovated by using bricks, tiles, asbestos sheets, but with the traditional pattern by using timber and planks. Most of such houses are being built with Government aid. The plinth area of the house is generally 10 ft. × 13 ft. There are two to three steps leading to the door way in height and mostly made of mud and in few cases of cement.

Social Institutions

"Kaja-Sahada" or the central street is an important portion of the Kuvi village, which enables the people to build houses in order to have a face to face living. In the middle of the village street "Gummam Wali" or Earth Goddess is installed. In every village there were bachelor's dormitories separately constructed for both boys and girls. Unmarried boys and girls spent their nights in their respective dormitories. Youth dormitory strengthened the social unity and cohesiveness and solidarity.

Its main social function was to impart training to youths in dance and music and the traditional lore of the Kuvi. Youth members were trained to direct their energy for successful adjustment with the people in social, economic, religious and other aspects of life. It provided sleeping accommodation for the unmarried boys and girls and was a store of all musical instruments. It provided a mechanism for initiating the growing generation of the Kuvis into their cultural heritage and the Kuvi dormitory was mainly a sort of matrimonial agency. Pre-marital sexual life is chiefly forbidden in the Kuvi society. But "*Dhunduni Pachhu*" song between boys and girls at the time of match-making before marriage was an interesting part of tribal youth. But unfortunately such an important social institution is gradually dying down for various reasons.

The Kuvis sometimes live in joint families but mostly nuclear families are preferred. A son after marriage goes to a separate house to stay. It is the usual practice. The family is patriarchal, where father controls the activities of the family. After his death, entire property of the family is divided into equal parts among the sons. Daughters do not have share over the property.

The Headman

The office of the headman is hereditary. Continuance of the post by a person also depends upon the physical and mental fitness of the person. He is the head of the traditional Panchayat at the village level and presides over in such Panchayat meetings.

Family Life, Marriage and Divorce

There are various ways of acquiring mates among them like, marriage by choice, arranged marriage, elopement and Gharjwaine etc. Boy's side pay bride price or *jholla* to get a girl in marriage. Marriage is a very important happening in the life cycle of the Kuvi.

The parents without a child can adopt a child. Both male and female may go for divorce at their will and can re-marry for the second time. Widow re-marriage is allowed among the Kuvis.

Political Life

The indigenous tribal communities still have well organized patterns of traditional leadership not only at the village level but also at the "*Mutha*" level. The "*Mutha*" is consisted of a group of adjoining villages and is treated as an administrative-*cum*-social unit. Each Kuvi village is a political unit having its own set of leaders. The headman or "*Naik*", religious headman "*Jani*" and "*Saunta*", the so called landlord of the village, and other senior members, and "*Barik*", the messenger constituted the traditional *panchayat.* Their posts are hereditary. Next to "*Jani*" and "*Saunta*", are "*Bejunis*" and "*Barika*". The "*Barika*", village messenger, belongs to "Domb" or "Pano" community. Only the post of *Barika* is remunerative and all other posts are honorary.

Besides, the above traditional leaders, there were socio-religious functionaries like "*Bejunis*" female (Priests) and "*Dishari*" (Astrologer) who also held key positions at the village level of the Kuvi.

After the introduction of statutory Panchayats, the traditional leadership is gradually loosing its importance. The PRI members including Ward members, Sarapanch, Samiti members and Zilla Parishad members take part in the Planning and implementing processes at Panchayat, Block and District levels. They are responsible for the implementation of welfare programmes in the rural areas. However, traditional village councils still play an important role in deciding cases, like family and social conflicts, deciding dates for socio-religious festivals and community activities etc.

Household Furniture and Articles

A careful look at the Kuvi house gives an indication of the use of simple equipments. These constitute gourd, wood, bamboo and stone articles, besides baskets, earthen pots and iron implements made by the "*lohar*" or "*Rohali*". The '*Rohali*' are a cultural sub-group of the Kuvi. They make agricultural implements, like ploughshares, spades, axe, and arrow heads. The hunting implements, like arrow, bow, big sticks are kept in the houses and used as and when necessary. Small clappers, Dung-Dunga, Mouth-organ and flute are some of the musical instruments used by the Kuvi. Apart from the common materials to be found in a house, sometimes variations are marked in the houses of well-to-do people.

Dress and Ornaments

The Kuvis wear very simple dress that is sometimes not sufficient to protect him/her from extreme climates. Most of them use only Loin clothes. The women wear two pieces of clothes, one around the waist up to the knees and another for the upper portion of the body. A 'Dongria Kuvi' male puts on a cloth called *Kodi,* 16 feet in length and one feet in width. Some of the sophisticated Kuvis in recent times have started wearing *lungi*, shirts and full pants. On special occasion head-gear is used. Coloured turban is used by the groom during marriage.

Kuvi women are very fond of ornaments. They beautify themselves with hair pins, earrings, nose rings and necklaces. Wristlets and ear-rings are used by the males of the primitive sections of the Kuvi community. The males too, like to grow long hair and tie these into a knot at their nape in a traditional fashion. Except the Dongria Kuvis other Kuvi tattoo their faces and hands. A knife and an axe are inseparable companion of male Dongria Kuvi.

Food and Drinks

The staple food of Kuvi is *Ragi* (*Elensine Coracanal Gaortn*) gruel. *Ragi* is a major produce in the sphere of agriculture. It is cultivated in large scale by them. Gradually, Kuvis were motivated to grow rice. Now-a-days, most of the 'Kuvis' prefer to take rice for dinner and lunch. They cultivate, purchase and even barter rice from non-tribals and to some extent, from the Civil Supply Department Stores of State Government. Besides their staple food, the Kuvis consume a variety of edible seasonal products like sweet potato, little millet, vegetables, banana, mango, jackfruit and maize. They also supplement their food through various edible roots or "*Kanda*". During the joyful events, rice and meat are the most common items.

The 'Kuvis' are very fond of alcoholic drinks and narcotics. They have earned a name for preparation of variety of drinks, like 'Pansi Kadu' (Prepared out of fermented Jack fruit juice), "Salap Kadu" (Sagopalm toddy), Irpi Kadu (distilled *Mahua* Liquor), "Landa" (*Ragi*-beer) and "Pendum" (Rice-beer). Among the narcotics, they are very fond of taking tobacco that is chewed in the form of powder and smoked.

Religious Faiths and Festivals

The Kuvis believe in "Dharti Penu" or Earth Goddess as the Supreme Being. She is all-powerful and is regarded as the highest of all deities. Therefore, she is, worshipped in all the ceremonies as a mark of honour and respect. "Gummam wali", "Jhakiri", "Sunukudi", and "Jatrakudi" are common places of worship in almost all Kuvi villages at different occasions. Gungi Penu, Bhima Penu, Lai Penu and Sita Penu are the deities of stream, hill, forest and wealth respectively. Birna Penu is responsible for rain. Sun is worshipped as 'Dharmu Devata'. They also worship ancestor spirits called the "Dumas". They believe in the existence of Ghosts known as "Mahani". They also believe in and practice white and black magic.

The Kuvis prefer to have a large number of feasts and festivals round the year. The religious ceremonies and festivals are "Herei Parbu", and "Setra Beta". "Bicha Parbu", "Mandiarani", "Pusu Parbu, "Harti Puja", "Sita Puja" and "Meriah" or "Toki Parbu". Toki Parbu is observed in the month of February-March with pomp and gaiety.

Health and Hygiene

The Kuvi people have very poor sense of hygiene and sanitation. The poor living condition and lack of awareness about personal hygiene are the factors responsible for their poor health. This results in skin and other infectious diseases. They do not take bath properly and the teeth are not properly cleaned. Many of them wear dirty clothes and use mainly water of the stream and generally they do not prefer to use tube-well water even though now-a-days tube wells are dug in the villages. The Kuvis have a peculiar psychology that flow water is better than any type of stagnant water. Therefore, they suffer from water borne diseases, like diarrhoea, dysentery and other gastrointestinal diseases. The diseases like tuberculosis, influenza, cold and cough are also common among the Kuvis. They also suffer from Malaria frequently, which is one of the major causes of untimely death of the tribals. Most of them believe that the diseases are caused by evil-spirits or "Dumas" and they prefer to go to "Bejunis" and "gurus" rather than to doctors and other health workers for treatment.

Life Cycle of the Kuvi

Below is given a brief analysis about the life cycle rituals of the Kuvi.

Birth

Birth occasion rejoices every body in Kuvi community. They think that it is a moment when an ancestor takes rebirth and gets back to life. The rebirth of an ancestor is definitely a mark of future prosperity. The joy starts from the moment when a woman gets pregnant. Women play multiple roles as livelihood earners, child bearers as well as child rearers. A woman, right from the conception until the last month before delivery, works in the fields and does other domestic works. She is neither specially cared for nor neglected during pregnancy. However, she tries to keep herself active.

When labour pain begins, some women massage oil of "*Mahua*" seeds or castor seeds on the abdomen. Such gentle massage continues till child's birth. The 'Placenta' is buried behind the house after delivery. After birth, the mother and the child are given a place in '*dapa*' for a month. The pollution period is to be observed for one month. During this period, the mother is restricted to move into other rooms and also to move in front of 'Dharani Penu'. She is provided with very light food, like hot cooked rice, salt and *raggi* gruel. At the end of pollution period both the mother and the child are given purification bath with turmeric and mango bark paste.

After the home entry, another religious performance is observed and the child is given a name. When the name is given, the performer offers a sacrifice to satisfy the ancestral spirits. The sacrificial animal may be a pigeon, a fowl, a goat or a buffalo depending upon the economic status of the family concerned.

Marriage

In marriage, the Kuvis maintain endogamy. The types of marriages generally observed are arranged marriage, marriage by elopement, marriage by force and remarriage. In any type of marriage girl's decision is final. The husbands are generally older than wives. Among the Kuvis, like other tribals, there is the system of bride price in which the boys' side gives some cash, ornament, crops, cloth and cow, liquor etc. to girls' parents. They consider a girl as the daughter of their "*Kutumba*" (lineage). Hence, the marriage ceremony takes the shape of a community festival. This bride price varies from place to place. Those who are not able to pay are asked to work in the house of his would be father-in-law until his bride price is thought to be paid. This is known as "Karjami". Both Levirate and sorate type of marriages are prevalent in their society. Polygyny is accepted in all circumstances. Widows may remarry. Some of the advanced sections of the Kuvi community in recent time have started imitating to certain extent the Hindu form of marriage.

Death

During deaths, the Kuvis practise cremation but burial is also done when death is due to infectious diseases. The death rites are meant for the appeasement of the spirit (*dumba*) in the other world. In this performance, mango bark is used as the purification material. In normal death, the corpse is not touched by those who are not a relative to the person. The corpse is carried to the cremation ground on a cot (*Kateli*) or a bamboo mat. On reaching the cremation ground the corpse is dressed with new clothes brought by the relatives. In each village the cremation ground is somewhere in the nearby forest. Well to do families may organize a feast for the people who participate in the funeral rites. "Hakki Kadu" (wine for the hunger) is to be provided. Those who attended "Mahani" (cremation ground) will be purified after bathing "Maha eau" which act is performed by the village priests or *bejunis*. After death, it is believed that they will go to sphere of "*Jamarani*", the goddess who created the earth. They believe in rebirth.

Inter-ethnic Relationship

The ethnic group closest to the Kuvi and in constant touch with their socio-economic life are the "*Dom*" (Scheduled Caste). They have been co-setting with Kuvi since long. Doms serve Kuvi as a *barik* (the messenger) and assist during trading. Apart from *Doms*, we come across a local caste Hindu community people known as the "*Sundhis*". They were wine venders in tribal areas. Their trading in liquor has considerably reduced in recent times. They have started trading in various other things in Kuvi areas. The *Sundhis* are now found to deal with cooked food items, snacks etc. in the weekly markets. Some of them work also as money lenders. Other castes of plains, other than "*Sundhis*" and "*Doms*" are the "*Kaini Jati*". They have also inter-ethnic relationship with Kuvis.

Hindu festivals like '*Rath Yatra*', '*Dusherra*', '*Ganesh Puja*', *Dewali* etc. are some of the socio-religious functions which bring Kuvis and other caste Hindus to common platform. It is called as 'Sanskritization'/ 'Aryanization'/'Hinduization' of Kuvi by anthropologists and others.

Socio-economic Life

The Kuvis are backward both educationally and economically. They mostly live in the hills and forests away from the main stream of civilization. They have inadequate access to natural resources endowments. Cultivation (mostly shifting cultivation) is not able to provide a Kuvi family food for the whole year. The yield rate of the hill type of cultivation is quite low. So, they supplement their food requirements through food gathering like collecting various roots, fruits, flowers and leaves to eat and survive. As mentioned earlier their health condition is very bad. They suffer from various diseases. Educationally, they are far behind. Poor and subsistence economy does not permit them to send their child to school for education. Most of them live below the Poverty line. Lack of education and awareness, simplicity and poverty make their economy exploited. They are exploited in the hands of the money lenders, traders, middle man, wine vendors etc. At the same time some of the unscrupulous Government officials do not hesitate to exploit them. So, their socio-economic life remains precarious and miserable.

Development and Change

With the passage of time and in the era of Planning, some transformation has been noticed among the Kuvi in Odisha. This was, more or less, on account of development of communication, transport, education, enactment of some protective laws as per the provisions of the Constitution of India. A small number of Kuvis have marginally gained because of various welfare measures undertaken during the plan period. But majority of them living mostly in remote areas, in the hills and forests have not gained much economically and socially even after so many years of planning. Hence, further sincere efforts are required to make the development schemes reach the tribes in general and that of the Kuvi in particular. They must be empowered enough both socially and economically through various measures by the Governmental and Non-governmental agencies, which would lead to their sustainable development. Panchayati Raj Institutions are gradually gaining ground in Kuvi areas, more particularly after implementation of PESA Act. Efforts are being made to empower the tribes politically. Although economic and political transformations are gradually taking place in Kuvi areas, these tribes are still interested to uphold their traditional culture including their folklore.

4

SOCIO-ECONOMIC IMPORTANCE OF THE KUVI FOLKLORE: A SAMPLE STUDY

Folk forms of the Kuvi may be characterized by their simplicity and spontaneity. These forms arise from, and are part of, the living life of the performers. Folk forms are the artistic expression of the people. They are produced by them orally and relate to peoples sharing a sense of belongingness with the same community.

Folklore of the Kuvi is not a fossilized thing of the hoary past. Its evolution is a continuous process and therefore, can become a vehicle of people's aspirations, anxieties, joys and sorrows arising out of their lived experience. From the very dawn of human society, man has tried to explain the mysteries of creation of the world and that of human beings by means of stories. The scholar thereby intended to throw some light on the inexplicable phenomena by weaving tales round the Kuvis (Kandhas) to satisfy the hunger for knowledge. The folklore of the Kuvi might unfold inner feelings of the Kuvi mind and make us to know about how they think and feel in the presence of the baffling mysteries of the world and how they interpret them.

In this Chapter, an attempt has been made to highlight the folklore of the Kuvi of Laxmipur block of Koraput District. Laxmipur is a tribal dominated block. About 90 per cent of the tribals of the block are the Kuvis.

Myth of the Origin of Kuvi Tribe

The Kuvis believe, strongly in the existence and impact of Supernatural beings or "Pennu" or "*dharmu*". He who "*talar'e dhariti tayamane, up're dharmu ductha mane*". It means he who pressed the earth and lifted the sky above otherwise both the sky and the earth would have been dashed. So, it is the God who made us possible to live on the earth.

The Kuvis believe that at the time of creation, the earth did not exist. There were no hills, forests, human beings and animals. There was full of darkness of all-round. Life of human beings emerged in the bowels of the earth, from which they found it difficult to come out. As per their myth, the original place of their birth was below 'Sapangada' the cosmic hole from where all life evolved. It is believed that 'Jamarani', the ancestral mother of Kuvis, led them out of there.

Myth of Origin

The story runs like this in Kuvi dialect:

"*Desa aepi kini puspuni*" or "*leka donga Kata*" (Semili Boat Story)

Oke Kalata Loku besi ahi'lea mahapuru kalao budwo, juga budwo kihamche. ea' welata miniyaka taiye tangiye desa aepi kittu inji e'a puspuni mane.

Oke kalata ke' set'ra beta hajili taki, guda pada nato'ti Loku'n, hatti kiwi ate'. Eda' taki' guda pada beta hajili hache'ru. Beta' Lusili taki ewaru ra jadata hacheru. Beta' Lusi Lusi echaka echaka horru maddi'n hochin' hochin' hacheru. Ewa at'u — dumba Adu, piridi ada, pipidi ada, basubeti sua ode Lodini Sua.

Lodini Sua e'ni puta taki we'da dadi achimache. Achiputa titi katra bati katra kuruhu, eyu undili hu'ata wahamache. Ed'aa mesa'na ra' baniyan amb'u pu'nditi'n. Ea talli kruhun bandita machi kruhun dalu ea baniyan tale hada atti'n. Ea giyan ambiti wahimjane inji baniyan ben'ga aahanchi. Sinikini Putataki Kuruhu dal'u aaya bandi bitra tiea hada aahimne. kuruhu dalu weste.

"*Ma aaya ode nange enataki payadee? Juga budwo, kala budwo bela wahimjane. Aaiye nanuea Punjamjanabu. Maro ode ri' dinatiea sabu janata ha'no. Aambai ode em'ba doyau. Ei' horru wali, mar'mun Kanda, go'cha gu'chu ode Pot'a Kati So'bun gu'npunne. Mambu dharmu deveta tiye ea' ka'ta wenjamjanabu.*"

Ei Kat'a wenjana baniyn Kabb'a ahachi'n. Kuruhu dal'u ode weste "ninu an'a on'fana'n. manga Paya' Sariye embati nidili taki jiru westain". Embati Pundani am'bu baniya'n eata tuti'n.

Kuruhu da'lu bewest'e "ninu'n begi nat'o halamu, embatiye semili donga, Le'ka donga tale donga Pekamun."

Eda' wenjisohe' baniya'n tame ija' hachiyn'u ode sob'e Kat'ha tana', tangi westatiyu'n. Kruhu dal'u westilehe'n ki donga kepitiyn'u.

Kuruhu westi lehe'nki surugudu kambriyu'n, lekera pekera Lahariyu'n, Raimani taspa, Rukamani bindhna, bijamari tengia, Raibina

Katilli ei' sabu tale atha di'na upasa n'a dina baida dayana ea donga kepitiyun.

Ei kat'a natati sab'u lo'ku ki wesiliye tana tangi pisana, ambaru kat'a man'wa aa'ateru. Kotra kat'a rondi asana ewaiy'n eala kihamjane inji kaki'teru.

Kuruhu weheni lehe'n Sanibara hajji Adibara wahi juga buduo desa buduo ahili mathite. Tai tangiki weste "jemu bandu jemu tangi kutna, ruchna kimmu". Tangi weste "hajjnein wahine begin paara, sanda paara, weshka parei'n iche". Ambati tai tangi pishpi aa'ane donga bittri hadgatu. Tama tale tam'aa tinee kadi kanda, da'ka, tini puti battiya, ra puti jayu, roshana danga ta hattu ode dangoti dara sunditu.

Juga buduwa wela wahilein, piyuu matthite, Satta dina, satta rati, piyu pih'aanae rite. Ei bumita sabu waki eyu meshili a'te. Saarga bima, mindi bima, bada bima piyu riee kiteru.

Ode do'ye wahana taade maati upre saagada tale piyu eyu tale pata weteyun. Merki magaa/satta bisa so'guta, hargimundiya nangli taadi mutta hemburi, sapa maarmu kapru, satta hata marchu, mama banja kodi tale pa'ta weteru. Juga budwa aahilean endi jaka dayatede.

Embatie Bimien Mireinki guda angaa pidka aatu. Bimiyus onphittiyun ei sabbe papo nango lagana na mirein ila atti inji mahapru ki wesili haacin. Mahapru tana bana' rettin ode ebana'ki ra kawa kittin. Embatie kawa ki jiyu hihana neethite'. Mahapru kawa ki wesha panditi imbia nara nidamneriki hengamu. Embatie kawa uda a'hin sabu jaaga sinni kiwi rette. Embatie ra tana leka donga meshte. Mahapru ela inji kawa weshkache. Mahapru kawa wechi'n "embaa aamba aambai mannu"? Kaawa weshte saari suttu sutki aahajamnu. Eda taaki hendili pan'aate. Mahapru eda taaki tanna huppa tale ra baunra wihan kitti ade kawa tale pandite. Ea baunra wihan hajjana dangota ra kani kitte. Kani aahile, dangdta maniloku, kani attu inji juta aku sunkittu. Ea aku kawa kathi gutita asana Mahapru tana waate. Mahapru ea'juta aku hudili weshtatin. Eda hudile Bima mirinti pidka dullachu ode ewain nehi aahanchi. Eda hendana Bima ode ileti piyu tale echen juga budua ki'on inji paramana kithiyun.

Embati Mahapru lekadangata manariki hatikithiyun ode ewari tai tangi maaneri inji puchi. Ewari tale eniki nara loku epi kiein inji tai tangi aangata attu aaya aaha tuppe ichiyun.

Attu aa'ya ahileea taiye tangiye punbi a'atude, ode judwi jadwa attu. Embatiea miniaka tai tangi tale'a baara jaana padi pada attu. Ewa sikka'nki ode Mahapru attu aa'ya kitiyun. Embatie ewari jakala punbi a'ana judwi jaadwa attu. Ewa sikka'nki, atte, sabbu adupundriki rakama rakama hadda hitinyun. Embatie aambai ambratale hadda a'wi a'hili ada'atude. Tambu tambue alga'ahaana we're we'reti jaati attu ode bihasoda ahi naraloku ephiattu.

Darmu Devta karma an'kana saarisututhi eyu haa'gu kiha'tte. Le'nju Devta katipatta, jada jandu epi kitiyun, kawa pinga tale jandu jada a'rna awikitiyun.

English Version of "Leka Danga Kata": Semeli Boat Story (The Origin of Human Beings on Earth)

Long back, the earth became heavily populated. Sacrifices and crises were the order of the day. For this reason the God planned to destroy the entire universe including every living creature on it. The God decided to create a new one in place of it. Here follows the story (*Puspuni*) about how the Miniyaka brother and Sister started the new generation:

Long back, all the villagers were ordered by the village council to go for hunting in the month of *Chaitra*. This was known as the "Satra banta" in the Kuvi areas. In obedience to the decision of the village council, all the villagers gathered and entered into the forests. They roamed around the forests and covered hills like — Dumba adu, Paridi ada, Pipdi ada, Basu beti Sua and Lodni Sua.

When they arrived at Lodni Sua hill the sun was about to set in the west. While a hunter was passing through a river *ghat*, he saw an antelope drinking water from the stream. He took an arrow from his quiver, aimed at the animal. When he was about to shoot he heard a scream. A voice requested him to spare animal. He looked around but could see nobody. He suddenly realized that the voice was coming from the animal itself; the kid in her womb was talking to the hunter. He raised his bow and arrow in order to provoke the animal to speak again, the unborn kid then said:

> "why do you want to kill my mother and myself? This creation of which you are a part will be destroyed soon. My mother and I have known it. After two days we all will die. All the hills, forests, mountains, trees, crops, houses. Sheds and people will thus be destroyed. This we have listened from the Dharma Deveta."

After hearing this, the hunter shook with fear. He asked the antelope whether there was any way to escape from the destruction. The kid replied "If you will not kill us; then listen — make a boat (*donga*) using the wood of semeli tree and hide it. Don't spare it anywhere under any circumstances. The boat will float when the heavy flood would come. Take enough food and other necessaries with you to last for a long time". The exact day of disaster was mentioned. The Miniyaka hunter rushed back and narrated his experience to his sister. They searched for a big "Leka" or Semuli tree and constructed the boat and made required arrangements. After it both the brother and sister stepped into the boat. They also took sufficient food items and other necessaries for them.

Then the disaster occurred on the destined Saturday night. Heavy rain continued for seven days and nights. "Sarga Bhima", "Patada Bhima", "Mindi Bhima" and "Bada Bhima" (Gods of rain) were the cause of such rain. After heavy rain for seven days they lebelled the earth like a corn field.

For this sin, Bhima's son suffered from unknown disease and there were maggots in the sore. Bhima realized this is due to his deeds. So, he rushed to the God and prayed for rescue. After giving the matter some thought, the God tore some hair off his head and created a crow. He gave life to the crow and sent it in search of human beings. The crow flew far and wide and searched restlessly. Then it spotted the boat where the Miniyaka brother and Sister were inside there and he reported it to the God.

When God asked about the creatures that were inside the boat, the crow replied that the boat was closed from all angles and it becomes very difficult to know who were inside it. Then God created a fly and sent it with the crow. The fly made a hole in the entrance of coverings of the boat which were closed by the brother and sister with the leaves used for their lunch. Then the crow took these leaves to God by its beak. By the order of God those leaves were burnt and the smoke of it rescued Bhima's son from the disease or wound he was suffering.

God was happy when he found that human beings were alive and wished that more of them should live on earth. When God realized that they were brother and sister, he then made a plan. He ordered aa'tu aa'ya to inflict measles in them. With severity of measles both of them were disfigured and were unable to recognize each other.

Thereafter, both of them were sexually attracted to each other and stayed as couple. They gave birth to 12 children. Again they suffered from measles and smallpox and were disfigured. Some of them became black complexioned and some raddish. New more couples started living together. God also changed their language (Mode of Communication).

By the mercy of the sun all water dried-up and became clouds. The moon God created other creatures, trees and plants. By the stool of the crow grass and other corns grew up here and there.

Different couples with different colours, and languages scattered all over the earth and as a result different communities were created. Likewise, different communities with different colours of people led to procreation over generations and the Miniyaka brother and sister become the first man and woman of the present civilization.

So, the idea of common clan and common brotherhood (*Vasudhaiva Kutumbakam*) has been established by this myth about the origin of the Kuvis. Like this there are several myths found in Kuvi (Kanda) folklore.

Riddles of the Kuvis

Riddle is a piece of verse giving cryptic clues as to the identity of something which the hearer or reader is asked to name. These are the puzzling questions to be solved.

Some of the Kuvi Riddles are given below:

(i) *Kanga Mar'mu donga ichhea, pid'ska po'ta gud'du iche (Baja ode pej'ni)*
- A tree having vacuum within created sound, sparrow started dancing
  Answer: This refers to the drums and the village priest.

(ii) *Nada hil'ah ayu, ku'mbra hil'ah do'ka (Na'dia)*
- Water flowing without drain and a pot made up without the potter.
  Answer: Coconut

(iii) *Taka' piridi sarigota, miti miti rinda, poda poda rinda, godkabadia rondi, sona mohori rondi (Neho'di)*
- Four things to walk, twinkling two, flapping two, one cowheard stick, one golden pipe.
  Answer: Dog

(iv) *Erea' Ka'da Badiya' Paji (Ven'duri)*
- Castrated fleshy pig inside a stream.
  Answer: Tongue

(v) *Samda Le'oh Kumunda' (Gatli le'oh man'si)*
- Pumpkin Perched on a structured roof
  Answer: Man sleeping on bed.

(vi) *Pod'u hil'a man'ji (Ha'ru)*
- Rice without husk or covering
  Answer: Salt.

(vii) *Ko'di durane dawana hajan'e (kumunda)*

- The cow is sleeping while the rope is laying a long distance.
  Answer: Pumpkin.

(viii) *Tali' ta'na manga hajili ad'ine, manga ta'na tali' hajili adea' (doka' ode mun'ta)*

- The daughter can go nearer the mother but the mother can't go to the daughter.
  Answer: Big pot/container to keep water and small round pot used to lift water from the container.

(ix) *Che'di I'chhe sar'i ha'ne, d'rua i'chhe sar'i wa'ne (da'ra)*

- Tell him to go, he will go, ask him to come, he will come.
  Answer: Doors.

(x) *Gidu gidu'ta wal'si ko'ja (Pure'ni/Pule'ni)*

- By the side of streams, one finds the foot steps of the deity walsi.
  Answer: Naval spot.

(xi) *Eat'ki per'ne per'ne tan'a taite' kugi'ne (du'cha)*

- After doing the weeding, it returns back to its own place.
  Answer: Comb

(xii) *Ra' pada, penda' hamburika parane (Janha')*

- A single girl, covering her body with a lot of clothes.
  Answer: Maize

(xiii) *Kana' wina' jhumki tan'dali (Bad'ti)*

- A small mouse roaming hither and thither.
  Answer: A lamp.

(xiv) *Palka man'u wan'hi hile'a, har'a tich'e da'pie hile'a (dau'li)*

- She has teeth but no intenstine; she eats grass without discharging any dung.
  Answer: Sickle.

(xv) *Kaja' haru'ti sai'ni, pata trayun'ta wan'hi (Baditi)*

- Shed of a hill, intenstine placed above the bald head.
  Answer: Diya: Oil lamp in an earthen container with cotton thread as laminator.

(xvi) *Gocha' d'oye bach'a ko'di (hay'na)*

- Male calf under a tree.
  Answer: Brinjal.

(xvii) *Ra' Pada' Penda' Jetuni' hokine (Holu')*

- The girl brushing her teeth with bundle of stick brushes.
  Answer: Hearth.

(xviii) *Ra' Pada' duru' duru' pinga ghad'nea*

- A girl continuously deaficating with loose motion.
  Answer: Traditional grinder made of rounded stones (Grinding Stone).

(xix) *Jetere metere samanda Laoh' rinda kumunda'*

- Two pumpkins lying on the dense structure made up of braches.
  Answer: Dove eggs in the nest.

(xx) *Da'aa bela kad'ine, budhi bela dongine' (mir'sa)*

- She makes you burn in youth and bends herself down in old age.
  Answer: Chilli.

These riddles are generally asked by senior members to the juniors to test their thinking power and intelligence. These have great social relevance. Through exercise of riddles young persons come closer to each other. Riddles give them pleasure and amusement as well as are used for testing of their intelligence.

Proverbs of the Kuvis

Proverb is a sort of similar saying expressing a supposed truth or moral lesson. It is like a by word or saying that requires explanation. Here follows some of the proverbs of the Kuvis:

- *Hawan'an/Hamn'ba rate'a, Nana watea* (Elder sister came after completion of food/mainly rice).
  The important person has arrived after the completion of work.
- *Haten' de tedhi bias ra'nnu* (Back pain ends only after death).
  Problems will end with death of the person only.
- *Jon'a mache soi soi, Jon'a hil'ate ena soi.*
  If you possess maize with you then you are a friend.

If there is no maize, then what friend? It implies that there are friends with you till you have means to spend for them. No wealth, no friend.

- *Hazi Hazi Jiru dambite.*
  Returned from the half-way.
  It implies that a work could not be completed, left half way.
- *Bit'ri Bahari Nara.*
  A Person bearing the responsibility of all the works.

Generally, there are two bullocks while ploughing. The right hand side bullock is known as "Bahari Kodi" and Left hand side bullock known as "Bitri Kodi". Bitri and Bahari Kodi refers to the bullock who can shoulder the burden of the both sides.

- *Sor'ka ki ma ma'dey'a bad'iyu.*
  The pillars of our green fence are the strength of the thieves. As it is giving support to a thief to enter easily into the orchard.
- *Jahara tai'e bitti tinn'yin.*
  It is your own brother, who graps the entire property. It means main enemies are mostly our own people.
- *Dissra' pon'o, wih'an ban'a*
  The person who shows himself as an astrologer but does not do anything, just like the meeting of flies.
  Sarcastic comment to a person who shows himself as an omniscient, but he does know nothing.
- *Karma Saru/dukhia saru*
  A helpless person.
- *Kamma dandiya*
  A cheat/fraud.
- *Katt'a Kan'du*
  Chatter/Blaber: he who talks more.
- *Tinn'ba Kau*
  Bribe taker.
- *Koyu' Kenn'pu*
  Early in the morning; the time when the cock cries.
- *Wed'a dumm'be*
  The period of afternoon.
- *Panga'na laka ki wetti'yn, dori laka ki dru'iyni*
  A person committed a mistake and wants to appolise; politely says "I have not played black magic that can be returned back or it's not a straw that I can placate into a rope, I have committed a mistake, please pardon me."
- *Toy'ite pinga ho'ye, ir'te netru ho'ye*
  Just by stepping up you can can't soil, blood may not come out just by beating.
  It means you have to labour yourself to complete a work.
- *Aa'spa dri'pa katta'*
  The discussion regarding marriage by elopement.
- *Parrbu' ti'che saiki Loda, kaadni tiche bhaiki loda.*
  If you arrange a feast you will search a friend, if you are attacked by a tiger you will search your brother.

Friends are with you at the time of enjoyment, but the brother will stand by your side when you are in danger.

- *Nehi'n hara tan'a koddi mayili punau.*
  The cattle will not graze in a good grass field.
  When one is unwilling to work even in a favourable working condition (used as satire)
- *Koddi Lenguni — gori Lenguni.*
  Tail of a cow and another one is like tail of a goat.
  Feeling something uncomprable.
- *Ninu eniki nisini wedi, nanu aliki endi'n.*
  My dance will follow your rhythm of the drum. It means tit for tat.

The Kuvi Villages and their Socio-religious Functionaries

The Kuvi villages have characteristics of their own. They differ from the villages of other communities both in character and composition. The Kuvi settlements, more or less are conditioned by natural environments of hills and forest, their subsistence economy and specific traditions which are ideal for a tribal village to come up. The most obvious way to look at a Kuvi village is to take into account its geographical setting, settlement pattern and size on the one hand and the social settings including ethnic composition, on the other.

Most of the Kuvi villages of the sample block of Laxmipur are located in scattered manner amidst hills and forests. The Kuvi houses are constructed in rows and the space between two rows is the focal point of their socio-religious life where several sacred structures are found.

The geographical setting, settlement pattern and size of village are changing with the changing scenario. Due to large scale deforestation materials required for house construction are gradually declining and uniqueness of the Kuvi villages is gradually loosing its ground. Through planned development interventions now-a-days houses are provided through Indira Awas Yojana, and Mo-Kudia schemes etc. Hence, some changes are now noticed in their housing pattern. But the socio-religious aspects of Kuvi villages have not lost their ground. The traditional village institutions and the functionaries are still active in these villages. They uphold the tribal cultural traditions and folklores.

The Saunta

The Saunta is regarded as so called landlord of the traditional village although he is not the real owner of the lands. He distributes the land among the fellow tribals. Land actually belonged to the community. There was community ownership over all natural resources. Situations changed with settlement operations in which private ownership of land was established. But the Saunta plays an important role while distributing the dongar land used for shifting cultivation. The Kuvis never feel that the hill slopes belong to Government. They decide which side of the hill will be cultivated by whom in the current year.

Shifting cultivation areas are generally decided by the Saunta. The widows and the old aged persons get those areas laying in the middle surrounded by the lands of other co-villagers so that they can save their crops from wild animals. This shows the sympathy and help that the community renders to the helpless families. Such types of community support to individual families are fine examples of the Kuvi culture.

The Jani

The *Jani* is the religious head of the village. He is responsible for the performance of rituals and upkeeping of traditions at the village level. He is assisted by the '*Barik*' (generally a SC person) and other members of the village. He is the traditional functionary to maintain folk culture in Kuvi villages.

The Pata Pej'ni (The Head Priest)

Generally, one may notice about seven to eight priests living in a Kuvi village, but there is one chief priest known as "*Pata Pej'ni*". It is believed that they are instructed by the God through dream to become *Pej'ni*, in Kuvi villages.

It is interesting that neuter persons are generally ridiculed in other non-tribal communities, but it is believed by the Kuvi that they are specially sent by God to perform the work of Priests. Some of them become *Pata Pej'ni*. Their social status, therefore, is high in tribal folk culture.

Disra (Astrologer)

Dis'ra, the astrologer, may belong to the same or nearby village. He is capable of indentifying auspicious and inauspicious time/moment. He is one among other important religious heads of a Kuvi village. By observing the movement of stars and moon he can fix the auspicious time. He is consulted for every socio-religious rite and function of the Kuvi like birth, death, marriage, for eating new crops, fruits and for sowing seeds etc. He occupies an important position in the folk culture of the Kuvi.

Loh'riya (Black Smith)

For the repair and manufacture of agricultural implements made of iron the *Lohiriya* in a Kuvi village do have some traditional knowledge of using iron. Till today they do have importance in a tribal village and in every Kuvi village one blacksmith family lives. They are also Kuvis but remain as untouchables (only for food items). This is an example of service class as we find in caste based society.

Their services are remunerated annually by each family of the village. In some villages they enjoy some patches of low Paddy land (about one to two acres) for the maintenance.

Kumbri'yan (Potter)

In modern days, potters are gradually loosing their importance due to introduction of aluminum utensils and pots. During rituals Kuvis do not forget to buy earthenware pots (known as *Tandi, do'ka* etc.). Most of them use clay utensils for their cooking. In most of the villages the potters do not live among the Kuvis but they stay in nearby villages and often sell their clay utensils through barter system and sometimes for cash. It is also a service class to provide specialized goods in the line of tribe-caste continuum.

Maj Diyan (Drum Beaters)

Among the Kuvis two recognized drum-beaters are found, viz. one is for *dangara* (*changu*) another for *Lisini* (*dhol*). They are the most important persons during socio-religious festivals. They enjoyed some low paddy lands (given by Saunta) for their service. *Mohoria* (piper) from SC community (*Doms*) may assist them while beating the drums. In some villages people from SC community also serve the function of drum beaters. This is another example of inter-community interaction and dependence in socio-religious occasions.

Medri (Bamboo-smith)

Bamboo made goods and equipments are also part and parcel of the Kuvi daily life. These are also parts of their material culture. They generally use *hechi* (cleaner/lifter), *dalli* (big container), *Suruki* (small container) etc. in their daily life and during religious festivals. Similarly, like the potters they do not stay in Kuvi villages but stay in nearby villages and exchange their bamboo-products either through barter or for cash. SC people also sell these products as middle-men. This is another example of tribe caste interaction in Kuvi region.

Sacred Geography and Sacred Spots

The tribals, by and large, are animists so also the Kuvi. They ascribe life (soul) to a number of animate and inanimate objects. Each aspects of nature may it be the hills, forests, rivers, streams, groves, and even the earth, sky, Sun and Moon etc. are Gods and Goddesses for them.

The religious life of the Kuvis — there are several sacred structures which are the focal points of their religious life and important elements of their culture. Some of these are as follows:

Gummam Wali

This sacred spot is situated in the space between two rows of houses of the Kuvi village. She is the Goddess of diseases. Here the Kuvis with the help of *Pejnis* (priest) and *Jani* sacrifice chicken and Pigeon etc. It is believed that the Goddess Gummam wali wards off small-pox and other diseases if she is satisfied with the offerings of the villagers.

Sunu Kuddi

This is the altar of the Earth Goddess. It is situated within a fence of interwoven bamboo strips with a small thatched house like construction with slopping roofs and it is located in a nearby place of a Kuvi village. Generally, they sacrifice a he/she goat to please the Goddess popularly known as '*Suneli Puja*' in the month of *Maga* (*Magha*).

Jakari

This is another important sacred place where 7 to 12 flat stones are installed in different shapes in Kuvi villages. They offer cow and pig as sacrifice. It is believed that deity would protect the inhabitants and their livestock. This is the abode of *dharti penu* (earth goddess). Sacrifice of the "Mariah" (*toki Puja*) is performed here. In the long past human sacrifice was given for better crops, it is said. It has been banned now. As an alternative a buffalo is being sacrificed during "Mariah" festival. Tribal people forming mainly an agricultural community many such religious performances are observed for getting good crops.

Kajja'a Penu

Any place selected by the village priest to offer *Pujas* to the "*Bada Deveta*" (the Big God). During such occasion, buffalo is generally offered as sacrifice. No specific construction or stones are kept in such places. Often this is performed under a mango tree or inside the mango grove or at some other places near the village.

The Kuvi in particular are God fearing people. In order to get a good harvest for their survival or to protect them from natural calamities or dangerous diseases they generally try to please the Gods and Goddesses in charge of various departments. These are important aspects of their folk culture. Feasts, drinks, music and dances are performed during various rites and festivals. These are also the mirrors of folk culture.

The Deities: (pen'ka dorka) — Mostly Worshipped by the Kuvi

The following are the Gods and Goddesses mostly worshipped by the Kuvi on various occasions:

- *Badipuru, Gotimands, Sanosadari:* These are the deities to be invited first by the priests before going to recite the names of other Gods or Goddesses on any ceremonial occasion.
- *Gatapura, Gumapura:* These are the protectors of the inhabitants.
- *Sarga Bima, Patada Bima, Ajimaria, Bijimaria, Ranje Rudi tole:* These are the deities of rain.
- *Sitaraja, Lachminraja, Saji Hariti, Gulumi Harati, Tuti Harati:* They are the Gods of the wealth and prosperity.
- *Dharmuraja/Surujaraja:* He is the Sun God who witnesses the truth prevailing among the Kuvi.
- *Lai penu, Guma penu, Bijli amma, Sujeli amma* and many other deities are worshipped by the Kuvi.

Auspicious and Inauspicious Times

Kuvis are both religious and superstitious. Their auspicious movement, religious practices social functions are all guided by auspicious times and moments fixed by their astrologer (*dis'ra*). They do have nearly 30 *sogus* (such time/moments) which regulate their movement and activities. Here follows some of the important *sogus* of the Kuvi:

- *Sowing Seeds: Runi sogu/samanda sogu* are considered to be the best.
- *For the Planting rice and raggi: Ladd'a sogu* is considered as the best and they believe, "*Lada badda arn'a annu*" (means there will be heavy crop). But, another important thing is that the crop may be destroyed by the wild boars so precautions should be made to save the crops from being destroyed.
- To know the reason of health hazards (*di'yan wen'bi kiheli*): *Salpa Sogu.*
- To harvest *ragi* (*Mandi Hassili*): *Salpa Sogu.*
- To eat new crops: *Salpa Sogu.*
- To put scarecrow and Kutura in the midst of the crop field: *maga sogu*; it is believed that the tiger will protect the corn field from wild animals.
- To go for hunting: *Salpa Sogu.*
- For marriage: *Asani Sogu* and *Samanda Sogu* are considered to be the best moments.

Mudala Sogu and *Citra Sogu* are considered to be the inauspicious time and moments. Any work done during these periods will be a failure.

The Festivals

Observations of festivals are very important parts of tribal (Kuvi) culture. People go gay and enthusiastic during these festivals.

Here follows some of the important Kuvi festivals which keep them socially united and bring a feeling of togetherness.

Hire'i/Setra Parbu

New year of the Kuvi begins with this "*parab*" or festival. It is a celebration to welcome the New Year with joy and enthusiasm. Here the ancestors and the patron deities are invoked and worshipped. The members of the families sacrifice cocks during the *puja*. The famous "*Setra Beta*" (sacred hunt in the month of *Chaitra*) is observed during this festival. This communal hunt shows the strength and unity among the villagers. It is a platform where all the villagers gather and come together for about three days. They hunt any wild animal which come across in their way. If they can hunt an *elk* (*Sambara/Mayu'n*) it is a pride for the villagers. After bringing the dead body of the wild animal the real enjoyment begins. The village priets (*Pej'nis*) move around the animal with describing the Kuvi history, heroism, and strength and then it is offered to the earth goddess. Each and every family has an equal share of meat of the wild animal. The whole night is spent with dancing and singing. Another important feature of the Kuvi during this Parab (for nearly 8 days) they play holi with local made colours, mud, and turmeric water and also with *Phagu* (locally sold in the markets).

They equate the festival with that of the *Dussehra* celebrated by the Kings (the *Raja*) with the *Prajas*. They believe that they are elder brothers of the kings. Such a festival reminds the Kuvis (Kandhs) of their glorious past, their heroism and strength. The younger generations get inspired through these performances. The observances of these festivals are important elements of their folk culture.

Mandiarani

This is one of the important agricultural festivals of the Kuvis. This is generally celebrated during the month of *Asadha* (June-July). This is done before transplanting the small Peents (*tali*) of rice and ragi. No one of the Kuvi people is allowed to replant before the celebration of *Mandiarani* festival. The *Kaja deveta* is brought from the mango tree and some of the small plants of ragi and rice are brought to the village. They offer cock to the Kaja Penu and seek his blessings for a good harvest. The *disari* finds the day of celebration and accordingly the *Jani* of the village performs all the rituals. The *Jani* and *Pejuni* who perform the rituals do keep a fast until the end of the *Puja*. The festival is celebrated by each Kuvi family with pomp and ceremony and preparation has begun one month ahead.

Pidika Puja (Insect Puja)

Very often insects spoil standing crops. So during the month of *Bhadrab* (*Bandapana*) (August-September) *Pidika Puja* is celebrated. The Earth Goddess is worshipped to protect their crops from the attack of insects or *pidika*. This *puja* is not there in the calendar of the Kuvis; but if the crop is affected by the insect then they observe. Rituals are performed before the Earth Goddess.

Harati Puja

This is generally observed in the *Gundi* (*Phguna*) or in the *setra* (*Chaitra*) (March-April) month. This is a special offering to the God to fulfil any wish like curbing of diseases, for getting a male child or may be an offering after completion of any wish. This is done by a particular family with co-operation of the villagers religious specialists like *Pejenis, majniya, jani* and others. He-sheep, and peigon for sacrifice and seven varities of flowers, *gur*, banana, cloths, bamboo containers (*changdi, suruki*) and many other things are required for this *puja*. This is done by the side of roads of the villages.

Dagda Balani/Raksi Puja

It is believed by the tribals that the evil spirit or devil is moving all around. So, he must be offered sacrifice every year. Otherwise he may cause harm to the villagers. A bullock and coconuts, prepared food, wine etc. are offered to the devil. A clay idol of the devil or evil spirit is made at a place near the village. The *pejenis* opens its mouth and put rice, blood of the chicken, wine, coconut piece and then close its mouth and then open it after sometime and the offering rice is distributed among the villagers as *Prasad*. The rice is taken by the villagers and they mix it in the rice pots prepared for cooking by the family members and then it is eaten by all the members of the family for good-health. Animals are also sacrificed and Kuvis celebrate it as a common feast.

Bali Jatra

Bali Jatra is celebrated once in three years in *Barsi* (*Bhadrab*) *Lenju* (month) (August-September). The *Kaja penu* and Earth Goddess are worshipped. Every family gives a well decorated (with turmeric and rice flour) earthen pot (known as *tandi*) with an umbrella made of bamboo strips with some gur and a coin. The *Pata Pajni* gives seeds of maize to each family and they sow the seeds in the sand. Everyday the family members pour turmeric water on it so that the plants become yellowish. On the 8th day the villagers assemble with their maize plants and go to the *Kaja Pennu* with their "*tandis*" and offer cocks and all the members keep their '*tandi*' and umbrella before the *Kaja Penu*. The female members put these maize plants on their heads. After the festival ends, villagers collect rice and other things and celebrate it with a mass feast.

Germination of maize seeds indicates nature of crops production during the coming year.

Eating of New Crops (Nuakhaia) Festival (Parab)

Generally, this *Parab* (festival) is observed after the harvesting of new crops. It falls in the month of *Barsi* (*Bhadrab*). The *Jani* and *Pejnis* collect new rice and ragi and offer their gratitude to the Earth Goddess and keep these crops in a eight cornered small bamboo container (*suruki*). They pour blood of chicken and that is hanged in the middle roof of the *Jani* house. After celebration every member of the community eat new crops.

Koddi Parbu

The Kuvi rear various types of live stock including cows. During this festival they show their gratitude to the cows and they prepare a special dish of rice, pulses, roots and a small fish (if available) and offer the food to them. Each family (if possesses livestock) prepare the holy dish and serves to the cattle. Their legs were washed with turmeric water and the cow-yard boys collect all the cattle and by beating drums they take them to the middle of the village.

This is observed in the month of *Diyi Lenja* (*Kartik*). Cow herd boys are also offered a feast by the villagers. The cows or/and other domestic animals are important item of wealth for the Kuvis. They are engaged in agricultural operations. This festival is meant to show regard to such animals.

Jakri/Suneli Puja

The *Jak'ri* and *Sunukudi* of the villages are decorated in traditional fashion every year. In the *Panda* lenju (month of *Margasirsh*) (November-December) this puja is observed by sacrificing goat, chicken and pigeon etc. It is a type of gratitude and humble homage to the Earth Goddess by the Kuvis. The holy '*bono doka*' (new earthen pot) is used to prepare cooked food for the goddess.

Toki' Parabu (Meria Festival)

This is the biggest and expensive occasional festival of the Kuvi tribe. It is celebrated within a span of every 7/8 years. The main purpose of this festival is to appease the supreme Goddess, *Dharit Penu* and her disciples. To observe this festival, a decision is taken by the elders of the villages under the leadership of *Jani*, *Saunta* and other elders. It is said that long back the Kuvis were selecting a human being for "*Meria*" sacrifice, but now-a-days, as a substitute, a buffalo is used as "*Meria*".

The festival is observed in most of the Kuvi villages with pomp and ceremony. Preparation begins one year ahead. The *Jani* is assigned the duty to purchase the "*meria*" buffalo. It took a month to celebrate the function. Guests from other villages during this month come to each family. Singing, dancing, feast with wine and meat continue throughout the month.

On the final day of the festival just at the break of dawn, the animal is sacrificed and the first blow with axe is given by the *Jani*. Other blows fall one after the other on various parts of the animal and thus the animal is hacked to death. It is believed, more the animal is tortured more the *Pennu* is satisfied. This festival is observed in the honour of the Earth Goddess so that there would be good crops all-round.

Pusa Parab

Villages not observing *Toki' Parbu* observe *Pusa Parbu* in the *Pusa Lenju* (Pousha). In Laxmipur Block, villages situated to the Eastern part of Dharmaduar Ghat are observing "*Toki Parab*" and that villages situated towards western part observe another *puja* known as "*Sitidi Puja*".

All the festivals and celebrations are observed in the honour of various Gods and Goddesses, so that the tribal people get good crops, their cattle wealth would be disease free, the villages are saved from diseases and attack of the wild animals etc. Most of the festivals are observed on community basis. These are important aspects of their folk culture.

Folk Belief in the Use of Natural Resources

Mango Eating

Mango is one of the important fruits eaten by the tribes. "Mango" is an important food item of the Kuvi. They eat both green mangos as well as ripen mango. Later on, they take dried-up mango juice known as "*ambada*". They also cut and dry-up half-ripen mango known as "*champta*". Kuvis adopt many other methods of preserving mango for longer days. It serves as one of the main food-intakes for 3-4 months. They also mix the powder of mango kernel in the gruel prepared by them.

Mango is a seasonal fruit. It bears fruits once in a year. The Kuvis follow certain principles for the rational use of the fruit. These are the aspects of folklores to make proper use of such a useful fruit.

- They believe that eating mango before the seeds became hard results in wasting the fruits for that year. So, they have made it a principle that no body should eat mango before it has been offered to the Earth Goddess in the *Jakari*. They intentionally linger the time of observation of "*amba nuakhaia*" (eating of new mango), so that the mango in various forms can provide food support for a longer period.
- Nobody is allowed to climb on the tree or throw stones and sticks etc. at the tree in order to pluck mango before maturity. Everybody has to wait till the mango is ripened and falls on the ground. This tradition is followed so, that each and every person will have more or less equal share in getting the fruit, otherwise only able bodied persons may have lion's share. To achieve such a noble objective a religious touch has been given for *Amba Nuakhia*, i.e. eating mango after it is offered to the village deity.
- The Kuvis generally hesitate to cut any fruit bearing tree. Their folk culture supports this practice.

Traditional Principles Relating to Collection of Brooms

The Kuvis collect broom sticks from the hills or hill sides to prepare brooms. Sale of brooms supports their economy to certain extent. It is not only used for their household purposes, but by selling surplus brooms these tribals earn some income.

Brooms naturally grow on hills or hill sides. Nobody takes the pain to plant their seedlings. The seeds fall from the broom plants in a natural process and such plants grew-up in the rainy season. Naturally, if broom is harvested, before the seeds mature then it cannot maintain its cycle.

Here also folklore and folk culture come to play an important role The village council with the help of *Disra*, *Jani* and *Pejani* decides the auscipious time for harvesting of broom sticks. If anyone plucks the brooms before the fixed time, he/she is believed to be attacked by tiger or snake or will die due to thunder or lightening. Actually, the auspicious time for the harvest is fixed after the seeds mature.

In the appropriate and fixed time all the villagers go together to the hills or forests to collect broom sticks, so that all the members of the village community gets, more or less, an equal share.

Shifting Cultivation

Before starting of the operation of shifting cultivation or *podu chas*, the Kuvis offer *puja* to the *Horu Penu* (Hill God). They try to appease the Hill God with various offerings and sacrifices, so that there would be good crops and crops would not be destroyed by wild animals or birds.

These are some of the instances where the folklore, folk culture or tradition comes as effective measure for economic and rational use of natural resources. These are the unwritten rules contained in the folk culture or folklore for the welfare of human beings and protection of natural resources.

Folk Songs

Folk songs of the tribals contain great human values. These also have socio-economic and religious importance. Some such examples are narrated below:

Otamada bila seru, bori banda taleni
Kadata mane mayo tamberi, salaha minana namberi
Aya durupati re, aaya pidi ganga re
Kadata mane mayo tamberi, salaha minana namberi
Aaya sunukudi re, aaya Guma walire
Kadata mane mayo tamberi, salaha minana namberi
Aaya Budaraja re, aaya manika sarare
Kadata mane mayo tamberi, salaha minana namberi
Guda tile nanati, Pada bale nanati
Kadata mane mayo tamberi, salaha minana namberi
Jugo budow bela le, raji budow bela le
Kadata mane mayo tamberi, salaha minana namberi . . . .

Meaning

O Maiden, what are you doing in the Stream? Your elder sister is suffering from fever. She is at home. Do not waste your time unnecessarily. If you spend more time here, then who will do the works at home?

Our Deities are Durubpati, Pidiganga, Budharaja, and Manikasara. They are wearing beautiful ornaments like Sona Jhiliki, and Rupa Jhilikai (Gold and Silver ornaments). The sacred places of the village are Sunukudi, Guma wali, Horuwali etc. All of them regularly caution us that the time of destruction is coming soon, so we should be careful.

The moral of the folk song is that time is valuable; one should not spoil time unnecessarily. It also indicates that women shoulder greater responsibilities in family life. The song speaks of the deities and sacred places, surrounding the villages. The deities remind us that we should be careful and spend the time properly. The time of destruction is nearing.

Setra Parbu Song

Lori Ki Lori, Lori Lo lori
Lori Ki Lori, Lori Lo Lori
Eilaya'n Lori Lori Lo Lori
Alaya'n Lori Lori Lo Lori
Lori danguda Lori bulaide
Beta danguda beta bulaide
Amba Patara Jili Mili de
Limba patra Jili Mili de
Ache baile ache bal ayiya
Nai'n baile nai'n bal ayiya
Purba ra me'ra ke mangi aailu, purba ra niti ke mangi aailu.

Meaning

During "Setra Parabu" (a socio-religious ceremony) the Kuvis have a custom of begging from door to door. The song implies that's "We observe this festival just as Dussehara Parab is observed by the King. We beg from door to door. Do not think that we are beggars. Begging is not our Profession. We just beg to maintain our tradition. We do not compel you to give anything. If you have and you want to give, then give us. Otherwise say, no. We do not mind.

Oh, hunters! You can change your direction of hunting. The singers also change their song, the leaves of mango tree and neem tree are shining. . . . Let us enjoy.

Moral

The tribal people never beg. They live on the earnings of their own labour. During "*Setra Parabu*" they move from door to door and request people to give anything they can. It is just to uphold their own custom and traditions. It is just like gifts offered and exchanged during the *Dussahara* festival of the kings. The nature looks beautiful with shining new leafs of mango and neem trees. Let us enjoy.

Agricultural Song

Song 1

Wai'de soi waide
Kangu horu'ta hanade
Na pada emba mane
Sini kihan wana'de
Didi mad'i diyare
Pata Kadda re wa'ne
Atala hour Pasada
Kanga horru Kasada
Asada Wanede bopilo
Wamu'n Sabe Kama Kinode.

Meaning

Come friends! Come, let us go to the Pulses (*Kanga*) hill side, where pulses are to be sown. My daughter has already gone there. Let us go and see her there.

The stream (*Pata Kada*) is flowing from the hill (*didi madi*). The hill, other side of our hill where Pulses are to be sown, is comparatively flat. Bout our field is sloppy.

Oh, Maidan! The month of Asada (Ashadha) is coming. Hurry-up, Hurry-up . . . we had to complete the preparation of the field for sowing.

Theme of Song

Pulses are sown generally on hill slopes. The month of Asada is coming. It will come with rain. Before that the land must be prepared for sowing seeds. It indicates that the cultivater has to do the right work in right time. Agricultural operations cannot wait for anybody.

Song 2

Piyu rehi manjane
Dundura rehi manjane
Ala rani nedu
Ala bendiadu
Esika endaga manjana,
Esika Susuka manjana. . . .

Meaning

It's raining. The mist is falling on the ground. It is time for sowing seeds. Daughter-in-law, get seeds quickly. Don't sleep idle. Bring all our seeds quickly, let us go to the fields.

Moral

Seeds must be sown in the fields at the appropriate time. Women play active role in agricultural operations, so the daughter-in-law is asked to go to the field, with seeds to be sown.

Song 3

Salapa sogu tole harsu mattaa macheye,
Puyu Kode dalite, Padi riaate
Lodda sogu tole, Kuli uahaa Macheya
Kuli Kode aayate, Breha tinjatute.
Salapa sogu tole harsu mattaa macheye,
Puyu Kode dalite, Padi riaate
Bitiya sogu tole, harsu matt'aa machaye
Puyu Kode dailite, Padi riaate.
Salapa sogu tole harsu mattaa macheye,
Puyu Kode dalite, Padi riaate. . . .

Meaning

This song is sung not only for entertainment; but also it guides people regarding when and how they will sow the seeds and when they must do transplantation of paddy seedlings Salapa, Bitiya, Bitna, Jatti, Oya and some of other times are inauspicious times when the mustard seeds should not be sown. If the seeds are sown during such times then plants would not bear any fruits with seeds.

During "*Lada Sogu*" if anyone replants rice, the crop may be plenty, but wild boars will attack and destroy the corn.

So, this song guides the Kuvi to follow the auspicious time to sow mustard and other seeds. There are some auspicious and inauspicious times to be carefully followed by them. Likewise, there are a number of agricultural songs which guide the tribal farmers in course of their agricultural operations.

Song During Name Giving Ceremony (*doru itinati Pachu*)

Begi begi Pada aamuga talasa
Begi begi Pada aamuga nilasa
Ninga oya'in we
Ninga Jalay'in wa
Nitaki na jiyu, na taki ni jiyu.
Raha'n Kinawa, Sarda Kinawa
Doli to doli bapi to bapi
Ni doru tole tinji manabu Ka'u Kutha
Undi manabu Kayu jada . . . bapi to bopi
Rati taki, dina taki
Hasaw aana, kelaw aana
Bapi ninu begi begi Pada amu
Doyi tehe'n nanu nitaki
Katahin nanu bapi nitaki
Kuru takina ra'he'n, aambia hache'n rahe'n
Padda aamu bopi ninu jiyu mache'n
Keli Kina hasa Kina bopi
Ninu nange taki
Jiyu mache de jiwana
Mana mache'n de parana
Pada aamu bopi na'taki
Oyai'n bopi dinataki kalataki.

Meaning

It is the name giving ceremony of a baby girl. The name given to here is "Talasa". "Oh, Talasa! Grow up early. So that, I can take you with me. I can talk to you. My life is for you, your life is for me, Let us have fun . . . oh, my dear daughter! In your name we were eating the leg piece of the chicken. We are drinking chicken juice. . . . The whole night and day, we will laugh and we will play. . . . Let us walk together. Whenever and wherever we will go. . . . We will go together. . . . Grow up early my child! So that I can take you with me, I can play with you.

The Kuvi people so also other tribals, heartily welcome the birth of a girl child. This feeling is, sometimes lacking in the so called advanced non-tribal communities.

Ban'bi Kini Pachu (Lullaby)

Lullaby are sung to make a baby to stop crying and to sleep quietly. Here is an example of a lullaby:

Ho yahoo, ho ba ho
Maya ke maya, ma ba ke maba
Na sona, no puttaa
No sona dallu, na puttaa dalu
Uuwaiy'n dada ke, udike nanake
Wate kewate wate aba wate
Ho ya ho, sona ho
Daluke dallu, puttaake putta
Cachi wahimne ke, wi'han wahi maneke,
Cho' Puta cho, cho dona cho
Bai wahimne ke, soi wahi'n mane ke
Ho ya ho, ho ba ho
Cho' dhona cho'n cho'n putta cho'n
Khia'ba kai, khaiya k'aei
Budike buda dutcha maneke
Kairuke kodi potano'n.

Meaning

The Kuvis believe in rebirth. They think that the children are their ancestors. So, meaning of the song referred to is like this.

Oh . . . my baby you are my father, you are my mother, you are my male calf . . . ho ya ho . . . look. . . . Look . . . they are coming. . . . Don't cry. . . . You are like my male calf . . . ho, ya, ho your grandmother coming . . . your grandfather is coming. . . . Insects and flies are coming . . . ho ya ho . . . oh, my kid . . . you are my assest. . . . Don't do like this . . . don't cry. . . . Look, the old person lifted the old lady . . . there were cows, birds . . . ho ya ho. . . .

The tribals become very happy when a child is born. They believe that one of their ancestors has taken rebirth. They express their feelings and gratitudes to the ancestors, through the lullaby. Such songs make the child asleep.

Love Song 1

Ea bapi, jatara Pangata han'o, raha'n Kihan'a wano
Ea bapi, hukka hote nirasa, Lenju hote tarasa,
Ea bopi, Kadda aatala jiruta, mama nayu maneta
Ea bopi, tara tara hano'de, Paday'n sini Kiha wande
Ea bopi, e'da bela de wate, jaei go wamude

Meaning

"Oh Maiden!, Let us go to the mela. . . . Let us enjoy there. Oh my darling, full moon nights are the best, it enhances the spirit but the night stars are lazy. Oh . . . we will go beyond the streams, and mountains; where there is uncle's (in laws) house . . . be quick. . . . I am feeling drowsy. . . . Come soon.

The song is sung repeatedly and finally he insists the girl to go with him for love making. . . .

Dhunduni Pachu (Song of Matchmaking with 'Dundani')

Dundani is a traditional string instrument, very popular among Kuvi young men.

Dhunduni Song 2

Echi echi sardi bapiyo
Kumunda bando ta diyane. . . .
Talare kado bela tamayo. . . .
Kumuda bando ta diya ne. . . .
Upre mago bela tamayo
Kumuda bondo to diya ne. . . .
Gadi hache gada tamayo
Kumuda bondo ta diyane. . . .
Maro manoo bada tamayo
Kumuda bondo ta diyane. . . .
Soi re baie gahara ma yo. . . .
Kumuda bondo ta diyane. . . .
Ade bai gohara ma yo
Kumuda bondo ta diyane. . . .

Note

This song is a love song of the Kuvis of Laxmipur Block. Dhunduni Pachu is played with this song, without which the night will remain incomplete.

Meaning

Oh my small beautiful girl! You are like a pumpkin flower and your voice is like sound of the flute. The earth is below and clouds are above. . . . The vehicles are going to the towns; but we are in the fields . . . don't disclose our secrete love to others and I will also not disclose this love affairs to anybody else.

Dhunduni Song 3

Koddi madiyo re'yu ta, saba madi yo danda ta
Jada jandu nai re. . . .
Lidiki Licha yo Kandita, Pannki Wali yo dukuta
Jada Jandu nai ne. . . .
Mana macha ha yamumi, kasta macha ha yamuni
Jada jandu nai ne. . . .
Gara sansara Kinaga, duri Sansar Kinaga
Jada jandu nai ne. . . .
Kuti mudi'ne amude, kuti sarwi omu. . . .
Jada jandu nai ne. . . .

Note

The Kuvi always feel that forests and grass are very important in their life. So they desire that there should be more of forests and grass. Though it is a love song, it describes the importance of trees and grass and the forest.

Meaning

Let the Kodiya hill and Saba hill be covered with (trees) forest, bushes and grass. Let the old stones in the back yard be surrounded by grass and plants. . . . If you are willing, then come with me. . . . Let us make a sweet home . . . a sweet family . . . take a ring. . . . Take a saree. . . . Let the entire earth be full of grass and forest.

Marriage Song (Biaha Pachu)

Marriages are full of songs. Every moment in the marriage process is associated with song. Kuvi marriage are quite enjoyable as these are associated with a number of Songs.

Song 1

Jeai sarilo Kanjaya'n Pregano
Jeai ma judihey muskade pregana
Emni konati wadiga aw'aa le
Emni mula ti wadiga awaa le
Jail sarilo. . . . Jeai. . . .
Weda happu ti wayi go awa'le
Weda kanpu ti wayi go awa'le
Jaai sarilo. . . . Jeai. . . .
Kunja ma sandala kata'ya'n gatain
Mula ti golami takaya'n gatain
Jai sarilo. . . . Jeai. . . .
Eaniki itidi public awa le
Eniki itidi Rupeli awa le. . . .
Jai sarilo. . . . Jeai. . . .

Meaning

Oh darling ! oh my dear. . . . Come. . . . Let us go to drive away the monkeys with red and black faced. . . . Let us have fun and enjoyment.

From which side or corner our sister-in-law will come ? How our brother will keep her? He is, of course, rich, but Lazy one.

Song 2

Kaalu dusiyan wai'e de mam'on
He mam'on, nili koroti pisaha'n jamude de', eh'
Go'ndi brekhana wai'e de mam'on
Hemam'on, nili koroti. . . .
Kunja sala' ki Laja hileaa. . . .
Ea landu . . . , nili karati pisaha'n jamude. . . .
Munja sala ki laja hile aa. . . .
Ea landu. . . . Nili Korati. . . .
Kalu du'siyan. . . .

Meaning

Oh, father-in-law! Clean your feet and come . . . you have nothing to do. . . . Just leave your money purse . . . your son (Kunja, let) is shameless. . . . He is a lazy. . . . But if you leave your purse, then everything will be Okay.

There are a number of songs (both from bride's and groom's side), teasing each other from both the sides.

Pachu/Song (Kandna)

Also, the friends of the bride sing on behalf of the bride. These are sad songs expressing the broken heart of a girl while leaving her parent's house and going to her in-law's house.

Jail bailo Harare, jaei, adelo Harare
Haji mai'n de ade ho, wa'ni wara wai'nde
Eaniki posori aayai'n, eaniki soyeri aay'a, haji mai'n. . . .
Nana hingla padie'n, nana ada padi'en, haji mai'n. . . .
Sod'a chimbra aayate, soda aandara aayate, haji mai'n. . . .
Kando awa'n de adere, juro'n aa'nde bai go, haji mai'n. . . .
Amma sarilo aama ki, mama sarilo mamaki, haji mai'n. . . .
Baya kudolo gatai'n, baya ladolo getai'n, haji mai'n. . . .
Nara jekalo way'e lo, pido jekala way'e lo, haji mai'n. . . .

Meaning

"Oh friends ! I am now going, but I will come back again next week. . . . How can I forget you all ? The street, as well as the entire village will be silent. . . . Oh my dear! . . . don't cry. . . . I was nourished so affectionately. . . . How nobody will come . . . neither human beings nor insects will arrive our village after my departure. . . . But don't cry, I will come next week.

Such folk songs express their love, sorrow, affection, feeling and their emotions. The entire life and its happenings are narrated in such folk songs.

Death Songs (Hat'e Sari Dihili Pachu)

Aayi re Aa'ayi, aayare aaya
Ma ba re ma ba
Emeni Raji nimata, emani harsu bedata
Thana khihimnji, basa kihamnji

Ni dura goondaya, Ni Licha goondaya'n
Nidani minika ti. . . .
Suruj aaya tana, darmu aaya tana
Endi jangate, endi rejo ote,
Ni tasiya oda ha'n, ni rabiya oda
Aaya chadow aahamna, aaba chadow aahamna
Ambia pisa naha'n hachi
Dona re dona, aba re aba
Ni sahi sakala, ni pala khudah'n
Ni gare ha'n, bara bandan'a ejaha'n
Chadow aahan, melo aahan
Eaniki sahari aayai'n
Eaniki Pasori aayai'n
Emni tale pura hachi, emni upar desa hachi
aayi re aayi, aayare aaya ma be re ma ba
Wenawa bulow, oyanabu, wenawa dekha oyanabu
Ni handi kundi hin, ni chichi sipa suta
Baya pura hachi ki, Baya Baya aahi
Bulow aahimjadi.

Meaning

Oh my dear !. . . . Where have you settled ? . . . where have you gone ? are you settled in the valley or in the mustard field (the places where the crematoriums are made). . . . Who drought you. . . . Your corn field, clothes, utensils are missing you . . . how can we forget you' . . . you come, let us go to move we will show you different places . . . whether you have gone to the village of mads and you become mad . . . return back as my father. . . . As my mother. . . . Oh my dear. . . .

Note

The Kuvi like other tribals believe in rebirth. Deceased ancestors return back again in the guise of a new born. Souls of the dead always move around their successors. These souls are worshipped by them on various occasions.

Folk Stories (Puspini)

Story I: Gokii Ode Kawa Katta

Maha'n mara rondi mache Emba'n Kawa teba aahimchu, ro, dina besi piyu rite. Kawa nije illuta raha'n ke machu. Triki ki'n ra Goki wahana kawa'n ki weste, taie baie teru nang ichako jaga hiadu. Matra kawa ode Goki bitre Padea. Kawayai'n goki ki kothi kothi prerahtu ke. Goki trigi trigi marka pariti'n. ra bandi marmu korga'ta tirate. Embati Kaja piyu rite. Aaji rite. Waiye piyu rite. Laya piyu picileh'n Goki korga ti a hote ode hette, aaji'n ta sobe kawa hahajamnu. Gokii onkite nanga mahapuru rokya kiyate.

Eda taki — roie'n karma on'pate jahare wastam wane.

Crane and Crow Story

There was a mango tree where a group of crows were living. One day there was heavy rain. On the mango tree, the crows were happy in their sheds. But due to rain the crane needed shelter on the tree. The crows did not allow it to stay on the tree and by hurting sent it back. Crane felt very sorry and found another shelter for him. He entered into the cavity of a leafless tree. There was heavy rain with hailstorm in that night. The crows could not protect themselves from rain and storm under the leaf of the tree. The rain continued till the next morning. In the morning when the crane came out of the cavity of the tree he saw that all the crows were dead due to the hailstorm, but he was safe in the cavity. Crane thought it was the almighty who saved him.

Moral

If we do not help others when they are in danger, it may so happen that we may suffer ultimately.

Story II: Rat, Cat, Carb, Fish and Rope Story
Orli, bileyi, Kupi, mi'nu dori, rapi ode tengri puspuni

Ra nayu ta besi haki gateri burha burhi macheri ke. Ra dina burha kuna karga hacesi. Kunaya karhi machati kuna gaday'nu ta jinin'ga beta atiyu'n. Eada asana budhi'n tosakachi. Burhi edi anadi inji le burha idi jinin'ga kuha ichiyu'n. Eda ija itily ke burhi budrha haki aa'ateri ode baya aji ahyi'n teba aateri. Ea jining kopoli gatayi'n inji onkiteri.

Ro dina burha veska beta haja machiyu'n. Burhi ro'otiea machi bela ro babji batiyu'n. Burli manji ode ro taka hitiy'n. Manji ode taka guru kutiyu'n. Babaji besti'n hiheli mano mache, atu Leko mani jininga hiamu. Hiyate sari mi kota duverita hahi mai'n ichiyu'n. Burhi ena kiyi'n inji onkana atu lego tiya jinin'ga kodana babaji ki hiha de tuti'n.

Babaji eda asana hajatiyu'n. Burha wanati ijo enayi jakala hilate. Buruli dihana Kuga mache. Burha sabu katta wenjitiyu'n. Embati burha babaji tiye eda minja takayi'n inji hachi. Haji machati orli, bileyi, kupi, minu, rapi ode tengri jiruta beta ahana ewariki sobu kata westatin. Eda wenjana. Sobu burha tole wanobi itcheri.

Burha tole hajana orli ode bileyi babaji ijati atu lego hotu, kupi eyu dokata hote, minu holuta dori, dukuta ode rapi kota duverita hote. Tengri kona ta dugate. Orli jininga Karkite. Bileye eda angamache. Endi ela ahimne inji babaji nigiti. Hichu uki meh'in injini Putataki minu termibite. Mumbu rupi'n inji doka tiey eyu Kodinati Kupi Kachite. Pangata hote Laka rapi ta griste. Dori gaste, tengri haye we'te. Babaji hahade hachin. Ewari ea jininga asa wateri.

Jiru waja tinji macheri. Ea jining ita macheri. Ro ramana ea jining Perha Ote. Eni Kino Inji bichra aahmna beta Lusi teri. Berha rondi Payana, ra Kaja Paka wali ta iiteri. Berha tinji inji ramana wate. Ramana Payana jininga tachana burha hiyateri ode mambu ena kinabu iecheri.

Burha westi, bileyiti ninu nayuta manamu Kokri Podaki ita manani tinamu. Orli arna tinamu kupi minu kadata manju ichi'n. Rapi ilaka uspaperi ichi'n. Dori ninga inji che. Tengri ninu mansi tole doyidi burha ate sari ninu ode ro koda lehe'n kama kidi.

Burha wehni Lenh'n Sobe jana kama kihi maneri.

Meaning

An old man and old woman were living in a village. They were very poor. One day the man went to dig roots to eat. While he was digging roots he found a bell. He brought it and showed it to the old woman. Old woman asked him to know what it was. It was a strange thing for them. When they kept the bell in their house it was found to be very lucky for them. The old couple no longer felt hungry. They prospered.

One day the old man went to collect fire wood. The old woman was alone at home. At that time a mendicant came to beg. The old woman offered him some amount of rice and a one rupee coin. But the mendicant refused to accept these things. He said "if you really wish to give something to me, then give the bell you kept on the loft. Old woman was shocked. First she could not decide what to do. Finally, she made up her mind and gave the bell. The mendicant took it away. When old man returned she told everything to him and wept. Tears were rolling in her eyes. Old man listened everything and then he rushed to get the bell back from the mendicant.

While going on the road, the old man came across a rat, a crab, a fish, a stick, a rope and some dung. They all asked "where are you going old man?" Old man told them everything what had happened. After listening, the facts from the old man they told that they would come with him.

After reaching the person's house, the cat and rat went into the loft of the house and the crab entered into the wet pot. The fish entered into the fire place, the rope stayed on the Varandah, stick kept itself in a cornor of the house and the dung stayed at the door step. The rat gnawed the handle of the bell. The cat stopped it from falling down. The mendicant listened the sound and woke up. After getting up he lit the fire. The fish rolled about "I shall wash my face" the medicant said to himself. Then he went to the water pot. The crab bite him. "I shall go outside he said. Then he went outside. The dung caused him to slip, the rope tied him and the stick beat him.

The cat took the bell and gave it to the old man. They beat the mendicant to death.

After that, they went back. At one place they cooked food and were eating. A vulture came and lifted up the bell. Then all of them made a plan. They went for hunting. Lastly, they killed a wild boar and placed the dead animal on a big flat rock and could hide themselves. The vulture came to eat the boar. Then they killed the vulture and brought the bell back. Then they asked the old man to tell about what they would do further for him!

The old man said them one by one. To the cat he said, "you cat! Stay in the village and eat what the children put down. You rat! Eat grain and stay in the village, crab and fish! Both you live in the river. You dung! Let the people use you to plaster their houses. You rope will help people to tie for whenever needed, and then he said to the stick, to be with the man and become the third leg when they grew old. Then the old man returned with the bell.

The Kuvi folklore is full of imaginary stories. Their entire surroundings, including hills, forests, rivers, streams, the earth, the sun, the moon, and animals etc. all are the characters of their folk. These contain morals. They are narrated justifying their rituals and festivals. They guide their socio-cultural and religious activities. The Kuvis folk culture include their arts and crafts, folk artitecture, folk customs, folk cookery, recreation and games, folk medicine, folk religion and performing folk arts like folk drama, folk music, folk dance and many other things of folk forms.

Hence, the folklore of the Kuvi is the treasure house of innumerable tales, stories, songs, myths, puzzles and riddles etc. Folk songs narrate the inner feelings, love, sorrows, pain and pleasure of their heart. Folk tales narrate the greatness of their heroes, forefathers, deities and the nature. Folk dramas not only entertain the people but also narrate mythological stories containing morals. These were the unwritten literatures which had been coming down from generation to generation and communicated verbally through mouth and ears of the indigenous people. Now, efforts have been made in various spheres to keep a record of them through formal literary forms and audio-visual techniques. Only a few examples of folk literature have been narrated in this Chapter in order to meet the academic requirement of the scholar.

5

SUMMARY AND CONCLUSION

Folklore of the Kuvi is an important part of their culture. It is communicated through verbal or expressive literature and behaviours visible through the material life (including customs and rituals), performances and public displays of the individuals. It contains the whole gamut of the Kuvi society including their family life, economic structure, informal education, aesthetic and cultural values, religion and traditional political set-up. All these are reflected, guided and justified in their folklore. Of course, some changes or transformations have been noticed in the folk culture of the Kuvi due to their contact with non-tribal communities with the opening of Kuvi areas to outside world during recent times.

It is their folklore which has united the Kuvi as members of one family since time immemorial. Continuity of their rituals, traditions, beliefs, faiths and taboos etc. proved their authenticity and reliability through their folk culture. Impact of the so called modernization in the form of educational system, entry of the non-tribals into tribal areas, assimilation of tribes into the Hindu culture and influence of missionaries, modern administrative set-up, role of NGOs have their influences on the Kuvi and their changes on transformations have to come. No body can stop it, because culture is dynamic. In spite of such deliberate impacts, the tribes in general and that of the Kuvi in particular have maintained their core culture through folklore or folk literature. Some scholars opine that the tribes are adverse to any change, those may be social, economic or political. Their social and religious practices, myths and beliefs, morals and justifications behind such practices, their clan relations and community feelings are responsible for maintaining their core culture.

A Kuvi proverb says "*Haten de'tedli bias rahn'u*", it means one has to work till death. A man with back pain continues his work, and work will not stop. The Kuvis do have much regard to those persons who can work hard. They give respect to dignity of labour. They never discriminate works as high or low, prestigious or non-prestigious. To them all works are equal. They love to work and hate the "*Kama dondias*" (Lazy persons). Such types of human values are found in the folklore of the Kuvi.

Kuvis religiously follow their self-made traditional rules and regulations, their customs and traditions. Many of the folk songs, stories and dramas tell about their past history, heroism of their ancestors, greatness of their deities, Gods and Goddesses etc. They seek the blessings of their deities for the welfare of their community, for good harvest, for saving their people from the attack of wild animals; such noble thoughts are found in Kuvi folklore.

Verrier Elwin, the notable scholar on tribal studies, has quoted in his autobiography that, "much of the beauty of living still survives in the remote and distant hills, where dances and songs are a vital part of everyday living, where people speak and think freely, without fear or restraint. Our workers must ensure, therefore, that the good that is inherent in the institutions of the hill people is not tainted or substituted by practices that may be "modern" and "advanced", but are totally unsuited to their economy and the way of thinking. The hill man has, essentially, a clean, direct and healthy outlook; he is free, happily from the morbid complexes in dues by the unnatural life of the city folk" (Elwn, 1964).

Elwin in his autobiography further, comments "most of the essential values of my life have grown and developed out of my contact with the tribal people. They have influenced me more than I have influenced them. They have taught me the importance of happiness and the importance of simplicity. Their own attachment to colour and rhythm has found an immediate response in my own mind." He has always inspired and encouraged the tribal people to live in their natural surrounding of exceptional loveliness. He also further said "of all things, beauty must not be forgotten. Beauty, eternally renewed in every generation, undiscouraged by big business or bad taste. It is the most vital thing in the world and must triumph in the end. The hill people of India, itself a country which has always been dedicated to ideals of grace and loveliness, still have much beauty in their lives by desiring to preserve it. I have not been trying to check their progress in the modern world. I have been helping them to inspire that world." Verier Elwin, in his writings like "The Bondo Highlander" (1950), "The Religion of an Indian Tribe" (1955), or "The Philosophy of NEFA" (1950), "Tribal

Myths of Orissa" (2006) etc. has amply projected the human values that are contained in the tribal folklores.

As mentioned earlier, the folklore of the Kuvi is full of human values. They always experienced in their myths, stories, folk songs, riddles and proverbs the presence of the almighty. All elements of Nature, the Sun, the Moon, the Earth, the hills and the rivers and streams etc. are the embodiments of Gods and Goddesses. Their folklores are full of with the praises of such Gods and Goddesses. These people are grateful to their deities for all that they have been gifted by them. So, they have a number of songs, stories and myths in praise of them which have been transmitted through their oral lores.

The present study has been intended to document and record some of the important aspects folklore of the Kuvis including oral narratives like myths, songs, stories, riddles, proverbs etc. The important objective of the study was to find out the socio-economic elements and values contained in the folklores of the Kuvis. Folklores also vary from villages to villages and community to community. Therefore, it was not easy to document and record all of them properly. There are various myths regarding the origin of the earth and the human beings. Though it is differently narrated by folk singers or story tellers, their story line may remains the same.

Most of the Kuvis are instant poets and they can compose songs according to the need of the situation instantly. They generally use meaningless rhyme words like *"jai ma dumara", "nilasa", "talasa", "jiliki jipora", "Hey dumbara", "Sarilo"* etc. Their tunes and rhythems may change with time, age, space, groups etc. So, documenting such folk songs was not so simple an affair.

Riddles and proverbs are not only used to make the situation interesting but also to test the depth of intelligence and knowledge of a person who is asked to answer. Folktales are the stories where all the creatures and things are believed to talk, think and express their feelings. They are often told to show the greatness of their ancesters, Gods and Goddesses. They do possess cultural and human values and socio-economic importance. Their economic activities are regulated by their oral lores. Agricultural practices, forest collections, hunting, food gatherings and all other traditional livelihood occupations are associated with their folklores. These are projected in their folk songs, proverbs, riddles etc.

The Kuvi always feel elevated, when they identify themselves as "Kuvis" or Kandhs. It is a very important aspect of their culture. They feel proud to say that they are the elder brothers of the king. Somehow the younger brother could be able to capture power and ruled over them. The Kuvis are broad minded and allowed the younger brother to rule over the kingdom.

Even if the all mighty God has created human beings including the "Kuvis", but the Gods and Goddesses always expect Pujas and offerings from them. The Kuvis try their best to please the deities including the spirits and Dumas through their *Pujas*, offering and sacrifices.

The folklores of the Kuvis narrate about the dignity of labour. They work and eat. Other caste people depend upon them. They feel proud that they are workers. They hate laziness. *The first hypothesis taken in the study is "folklore of Kuvi tribe is an important element of their culture and plays an indispensable role in their socio-economic life" — is found to be still valid among the Kuvis.*

The folklores of the Kuvis are found to be an integral part of their culture. Their beliefs, rituals and traditions etc. are justified by their folklore and they are being guided by them. Of course, these people are being influenced by non-tribal communities like the caste Hindus of neighbouring Odia, Telugu and also by other communities living among themselves like SC (*Doms*), *Sundhis* etc. To some extent, there has been assimilation of cultures and influence of culture contacts. Some of the tribals have accepted other religious faiths like Christianity. In spite of these, the Kuvis have not forgotten their age old traditions and customs. They still follow them along with the new faiths to which they have been converted.

The second hypothesis was that the folklore of the Kuvis is gradually loosing its significance. From the study it was found out that such a presumption was not fully true. In the interior Kuvi villages the folklores still continue to keep up their importance. Modern civilization has not been able to bring any perceptible damage to the traditional folklore of the Kuvi. It may be because the interior Kuvi villages have not much been influenced by the so called modern civilization.

The third hypothesis was, "the folklores of Kuvis tribe contains in them high human values and have socio-economic importance. Such hypothesis is found to be valid one. Folktales about the origin of Kuvis teach them one thing that they belong to a particular clan, and hence, they are blood related. They must help each other at the time of need. This gives a feeling of fraternity and brotherhood. Such folktales also teach the Kuvis that the Almighty is powerful and several Gods and Goddesses as well as the spirits, souls or Dumas are always ready to help them when they are in difficulties. So, the tribal Kuvi worship various deities on various occasions. Most of the rituals and festivals are related to various agricultural and forest operations. So such occasions narrated in their folklores have great socio-economic importance to the Kuvi.

The fourth and last hypothesis was that the human values and social integrity contained in their folklore are still of educational importance not only for the concerned tribe but for the humanity at large. This assumption seems to be valid even in recent times. The human values involving dignity of labour, honesty and truthfulness which are found among the Kuvi people are amply justified by their folklores. In such a society an individual stands for the society and society/community helps an individual in times of difficulties. Laziness is hatred and hard work is praised through their folktales and songs. All these have educational importance for the younger generation. Youth dormitories, folk plays and dramas are the mediums through which such socio-economic values of life are imparted. The dignity of labour, treating all types of work equally, simplicity and honesty, showing respect to women in socio-economic spheres, cooperative labour etc. are some of the human values which the so-called civilized and modern men have to learn from the Kuvi people.

"Their hands may not be soft but, they serve with their heart, their lips may not be perfumed but, they speak the truth. They have very little to offer but, they offer everything they have, if asked for." The so-called civilized persons have many things to learn from such so called primitive people. Are these people really backward? In this context Varier Elwin's, statement is noteworthy, "who is backward — the simple honest tribesman or the merchant who exploits him? Who is backward the creative artist at her tribal loom, the gentle mother with her child among the hills, or the inventor of the atom bomb which may destroy her and all the world. Are these self-reliant, cooperative tribes really backward as against, the self-seeking, individualistic, crafty products of our industrial civilization?" (Quoted from the *Report of Special Multi Purpose Tribal Block Committee*, 19, Chapter III, p. 21).

Folklore of the Kuvi, is a medium through which the souls of Kuvis find their colourful expression. Their happiness and sorrow, love and frustration thoughts and emotion all find their right line place in their folk, literature. The folklore of the Kuvis contains in itself their unwritten record of socio-cultural life and it is the mirror of the Kuvi culture.

Folklore of the Kuvi acts as unifying force of their identity and uniqueness. Their cultural life revolves around their folklore.

One of the most important beliefs of the Kuvi may be "the existence of god, who is Almighty, the supreme power. One example is given below:

"Uppre dharmu dutchamanji talare dhariti toyamanji."

You (God)! You lifted the sky above otherwise, it might have fallen and pressed the earth by your feet, otherwise, it might have come-up and all the creatures might have been sandwitched between sky and earth. So, all the creatures including human beings are to be grateful to the God.

Their myth of origin describes that the almighty God has given life to all human beings. They all are brothers and sisters. It's the *Dharma deveta*, the God who has given human beings different colours, castes, languages etc. for which we are different from one another. The idea of "*Vasudhaiva Kutumbakam*" (Universal brotherhood) is inherent in such philosophy of the Kuvi.

They also cautioned, it is due to the population pressure and all related problems the God thinks to destroy the creation. In one of their folk songs (No. 1) they warn that the "*Juga budow bela*" and "*Kala budow Bela*" (time of destruction is coming). The ultimate moral behind it is that the life is short-death is inevitable. One must visualize his death which is the ultimate truth and act accordingly.

Their folk stories referred to earlier like "*Leko donga*" (the boat prepared by the brother) "*raimani taspa*" "*rukamani bindhna*", "*bijamari tangia*" (unique tools used for special occasion), are meant to glorify their dilect, culture and above all the richness of their literature. Evans Pritchard has rightly remarked: that "As we know Primitive Societies have just as long a history as our own and while they are less developed than our society in some respect they are more developed in others" (1992: 7).

The Kuvi in that respect most of the tribals, frame their own rules, regulations, custom and tradition and follow them in letter and spirit. It is unlike the so called civilized persons who frame rules mostly to break it. The dignity of labour, dedication to work and live within their own earnings, truthfulness, honesty and simplicity are some of the high human values which most of the so called civilized persons are yet to learn.

As mentioned earlier, folk stories of the Kuvi generally teach the moral of life. For example, in the story of 'crow and crane' they teach to be kind to others. Their stories generally generate interest, capture the imagination, and leave a sense of beautiful moral on the mind and heart of the listeners. Kuvi lore is a storehouse of stories (known as *Pusponi*). Kuvi language does not have a script of its own so the story is not regulated by any specific procedure and many a times it is met with some absured ending (like the second story) where cat, rat, crab, fish, dung, rope and stick (odd combination) ends up absurdly. Of course, some scholar may try to find some correlation of them. The old and experienced persons become the narrators and younger generation listens to them with delight.

Riddles and Proverbs are also found to be important constituents of the Kuvi folklore. Riddles are some type of questions designed to test ingenuity in giving answers or meaning. Proverb is short pithy saying in general use about person of thing that it is widely known. These are composed pertaining to plants, animals and some aspects of real life. The person who has to answer them must apply his intelligence, ingenuity and presence of mind.

Kuvis are animists. Their cultural and religious practices are guided by their belief on Gods, Goddesses, supernatural powers, *Dumas* and *Penus*. They ascribe life on all these powers. Their entire socio-economic activities do find rightful place in their socio-economic folklores.

Their songs are charged with vivid intensity. Often passionate experiences speak simply, quietly and without any concern to decorate or beautify their thoughts and feelings. The theme of their songs is universal and timeless like hill-streams and never diverted from basic human concern.

They follow certain customs in which some moments either auspicious or inauspicious to undertake an agricultural operation for example,

> "*getti sogu tole harsu matta mache'n*
> *Puyu Kode dalite paid riahte. . . .*"

The "*getti sogu*" is considered to be inauspicious to sow the mustard seeds in the field.

The occasions like birth, death, marriage, name giving ceremony, sowing seeds, harvesting, eating new crops, hunting etc., have their songs which are appropriate to their respective operations. Joys, sorrows, emotion, passion, love and frustrations etc. are expressed in their folklores. The images and symbols, rhythmic words are all taken from nature including mountains, streams, trees, animals, birds etc. The folk songs and dances help them to forget the troubles and difficulties of harsh sun rays during the summer, heavy rain and its inconveniences and biting cold etc.

Appropriate to different social and ritual occasions different songs are sung and different dances are performed. Dances and songs are integral parts of their life and are regarded as sources of enjoyment and relaxation. Different musical instruments, like flute, string instruments, drums, instruments creating sound effect are used as accompaniments of singing and dancing.

However, it is a matter of great concern that due to the increasing culture contacts from outside the original Kuvi has been gradually diluted. Their lores have been influenced by the neighbouring dominating culture and languages. Now-a-days, one may find many Odia and Telugu words finding place in their folklores. Younger generation is showing less interest in preserving their core culture. Still in interior Kuvi villages, it is observed during the field studies, the core contents of their folklores have not been much affected. But, as the culture and folklores of the Kuvi as well as that of other tribal communities have great values as well as socio-economic importance, they need to be preserved in a systematic manner.

Certain Recommendations

Here are some humble recommendations to preserve the rich Kuvi folklore:

- To reidentify the Kuvi cultural zones; the same tribe may possess different types of cultural practices and we notice variations in their, dances, folktales etc. such folklores need to be documented and preserved.
- The oral lores of the Kuvi have to be recorded in its original form and with proper documentations.
- Language being the most important means of communication as well as to establish rapport with the people, the officers and extension workers including teachers must possess a basic knowledge of the local dialect in order to communicate with local people effectively.

- The Zonal centres must have autonomy to document the folklores of the tribals systematically. These centres must work as institutes of research in the tribal culture.
- Scholars interested in doing research on tribal culture in general and folklores in particular should be given help and incentives by the Government.
- Encouragement through financial helps and other supports needs to be given through Zonal cultural centres for performing folk arts during the local festivals of the Kuvi and other tribes as well as for participating in Block, District and State level cultural festivals.

Conclusion

From the above analysis we come to the conclusion that the folklore of the Kuvi (as also other tribes) is the store house oral literature. It covers folk tales, myths, legends, folk songs, riddles, proverbs, folk speeches and stories. It also covers folk arts, like graphic arts and dances. Various aspects of their life such as their economic life, social life, conjugal life, sacred life, their thoughts, their cattle, poultry, vegetable and fruit are also amptly represented in their folklore, folk art and craft. It is the unwritten record and mirror of tribal (Kuvi) culture.

Folklores of Kuvi have great socio-economic importance. Folklore brings solidarity, continuity and consistency among the Kuvis. When a sacred tale is told, it is to justify the rituals and to regulate the conduct of the people. A legend may contribute to the building up of morals. The old Kuvi people feel elevated telling stories of their ancestors and try to educate their young generation. Folk songs and stories usually educate the young ones and bring discipline among them. These folk songs or folk tales incorporate morals among the general attitudes and principles, such as laziness, rebelliousness and snobbishness. Some of the verbal instructions are given through Kuvi folklores during marriage ceremonies to the boys and the girls getting marriage. Some forms of folklore are important means of applying social pressure and exercising social control. Many riddles of the Kuvi combine recreational and educational values. These are socially very significant and instructive. They may mention ecological names or contain references to historical events. Most of the Kuvi (Kandh) folklores are related to agricultural and forest operations which are the principal pillars of their economy.

The time has come to formally record and document these valuable folk literatures of the tribals in general and that of the Kuvi in particular. It is because these folklores not only have great socio-economic and religious importance, but also they contain a lot of human values.

PHOTOGRAPHS

Photo 1: "Gummam Walli" one of the Most Important Sacred Places of a Kuvi Village

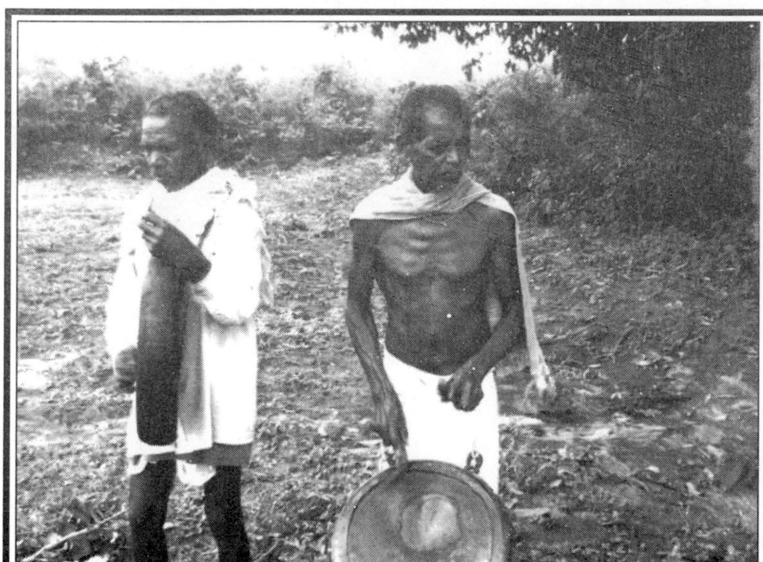

Photo 2: We are tired off . . . Our Future generation have to keep it up . . . shall they?

Photo 3: A Neuter of the Village Bandigar Narrating a Ballard with his String Instrument

Photo 4: I am Here to Follow the Rhythm of "Timiki" . . . Folklore will Never Die. . . .

Photo 5: "Marabila", Wild Fruit Used as an Musical Instrument for Effecting Sound

Photo 6: I am here to watch "Ambada" (A Sweet Pickle Made from Mango Pulp)

Photo 7: "Heka Marmu" is Socio-economically Related with the Lives of the "Kuvi"

Photo 8: Traditional "Sunu Kudi" with Modern Touch . . . Folk Culture in its Transition. . . .

Photo 9: Primitive Method of Preserving Turmeric Seeds

Photo 10: Sacred Hunt during "Setra Beta"

Photo 11: We are not Beggars . . . We Ask You Something Just to Maintain the Custom

Photo 12: The Investigator in a Kuvi Village Collecting Information

BIBLIOGRAPHY

Arnold, Matthew (1987). *Culture and Anarchy: Selected Prose*, Harmondsworth: Penguin.

Bailey, F.G. (1958). *Caste and the Economic Frontier*, India Branch, Oxford University Press.

Banerjee, Sukuman. *Anthrographic Study of Kui Kondha*, Anthropological Survey of India, Kolkata.

Behuria, N.C. (1965). *Final Report on the Major Settlement Operation in Koraput District (1964-82)*, Cuttack: Odisha Government Press.

Bell, R.C.S. (1945). *Orissa District Gazetteers, Koraput*, Cuttack: Orissa Government Press.

Best, John. W. (1982). *Methodology in Research*, New York: The Ronold Press.

Bose, N.K. (1971). *Tribal Life in India*, New Delhi: National Book Trust of India.

COATS, Koraput (2004-05). *Five Year Perspective Plan under NFFWP (2005-06 to 2009-10) Koraput District.*

Dandekar, V.M. and N. Rath (1971). *Poverty in India*, India School of Political Economy.

Das, P.K. (1975). "A Study of Some Aspects of Tribal Agriculture in Koraput District of Orissa", *Orissa Economic Journal*, July-December, BBSR.

Deogaonkar, G.G. (1980). *Problems of Development of Tribal Areas*, Delhi: Leela Devi Publications.

Directorate of Economics and Statistics, Odisha (2011). *District Statistical Hand Book*, Koraput, 2011.

Dundes, Alan (ed.) (1997). *Folklore: Critical Concepts in Literacy and Cultural Studies*, London: Routledge.

Elwin, Verrien (1943). *The Aboriginals*, London: Oxford University Press.

Elwin, Verrien (1944). "Notes on Kandh Tour", *Man in India*, Vol. 24 No. 1.

Elwin, Verrien (1950). *Bondo Highlender*, London: Oxford University Perss.

Elwin, Verrien (1955). *The Religion of an Indian Tribe*, London: Oxford University Press.

Elwin, Verrien (1964). *The Tribal World*, New Delhi: Oxford University Press.

Elwin, Verrien (2006). *Tribal Myths of Orissa*, Vols. I and II, Prafulla - Orissagarh, Ashram Patna, Jagatsinghpur.

Ghose, S.K. (1990). *Law Enforcement in Tribal Areas*, New Delhi: Asia Publishing House.

Ghose, Swapnajit (2007). *Sustainable Livelihood of Tribals Though Food Security Programme: A Study of Nabarangapur Block.*

Ghurey, G.S. (1959). *Scheduled Tribes*, Bombay.

Government of India (1977). *Approach to the Development in the Sixth Plan: A Priliminary Perspective Occasional Paper on Tribal Development No. 17*, New Delhi: Ministry of Home Affairs, pp. 99-100.

Green, Thomas (Ed.) (1997). *Folklore: An Encyclopedia of Belief, Customs, Tales, Music and Art*, California: Abc Clio.

Joyee, B. and Well, M. (1985). *Different Methods of Experimental Research*, IInd Edition, New Delhi: Prentice Hall of India Pvt. Limited.

Koul, Lokesh (1985). *The Research Methodology*, New Delhi: The Starting Pvt. Ltd.

Libenstein, H. (1957). *The Theory of Underemployment in Backward Economies*, Berkeley: Institute of Industrial Relations, University of California.

Majumdar, D.N. (1958). *The Eastern Anthropologist*, September-November, 1958.

Mann, R.S. (1981). *Nature, Man, Spirit Complex in Tribal India*, New Delhi: Concept Publishing Company Pvt. Ltd.

Mohanti, K.K., P.C. Mohapatro and J. Samal (2006). *Tribe of Koraput*, Council of Analytical Tribal Studies, D.N.K. Road, Koraput.

Mohapatro, P.C. (1980). *Strategy of Economic Development of Tribals a Backward District in a Backward State — A Regional Study of Economic Problems of Tribals of Koraput District*, Odisha.

Mohapatro, P.M. and Mohapatro, P.C. (1997). *Forest Management in Tribal Area: Forest Policy and People Participation*, New Delhi: Concept Publishing Company Pvt. Ltd.

Orissa Agricultural Statistics (2006-07). Directorate of Agriculture and Food Production, Bhubaneswar, Orissa.

Passi, B.K. Goel and Swanup, D.R. (1986). *Research Methodology and Socio-Economic Development of People of India — A Monograph*, Indore: D.A.P.U.

Patnaik, N. (1976). *Tribes and their Development — A Study of Two Tribal Development Blocks in Orissa*, Hyderabad, NIRD.

Patnaik, N. (1988). *The Kondh*, Tribal and Harijan Research-cum-Training Institute, H. & T.W. Department, Bhubaneswar, Orissa.

Patnaik, N. and P.S. Das Patnaik (1980). *The Kondha of Orissa*, Published by Tribal and Harijan Research-cum-Training Institute, BBSR.

Patnaik, Nityananda (1957-58). "Orissara Bivinna Prakara Kondhs (Oriya)", *Adibasi*, Vol. II, No. 4, pp. 26-31, THRTI, Bhubaneswar.

Patnaik, Nityananda (2002). *Folklore of Tribal Communities*, New Delhi: Gyan Publishing House.

Piaget, J. (1970). *The Science of Education and Research Methodology*, New York: Viking Press.

Piddington, R. (1956). *An Introduction to Social Anthropology*.

Rath, N. (1983). "Measuring Rural Unemployment in India: A Methodological Note", in P.R. Brahmananda and Others (Eds.), Vol. I, London: MacMillan Press.

Rout, Siba Prasad (1964-65). "Dom Exploitation in the Kondh villages of Koraput District", *Adibasi*, Vol. 6, No. 1, pp. 21-28, THRTI, Bhubaneswar.

Roy, S.C. (1922). "Ethnography in Old Official Records (Kondh Human Sacrifices)", *Man in India*, Vol. II, pp. 67-81, Man in India Office, Ranchi.

Samal, J. (1985). "Tribal Economy and Forest Ecology" in P.S.B. Rao (Ed.), *Tribals and Forest Eco-System*, Koraput: DAV College, Odisha.

Samal, J. (1985). "Tribal Economy: A Regional Study — A Case Study of Koraput District", *Orissa Economic Journal*, Vol. xviii, No. 1 and 2, BBSR.

Samal, J. (1979). *Problems of Tribal Agricultural in India*, M.Phil. Dissertation, University of Poona (GIPE) Unpublished.

Samal, J. (1992). *Some Aspect of Tribal Economy — A Case study of Koraput District*, Ph.D. Thesis Submitted to University of Poona (Unpublished).

Shanti, K. *Data Base on Rural Poverty Indicators*.

Shrivastava, B.N. (1968). *Exploitation in Tribal Areas*, New Delhi: Bharatiya Adimjati Sevak Sangh.

Singh, K.S. (Ed) (1982). *Economics of Tribes and their Transformation*, New Delhi: Concept Publishing Company Pvt. Ltd.

Singh, K.S. (1982). "Transformation of Tribal Society Integration *Vs.* Assimilation", *EPW*, Vol. XVII, No.33, August.

Taylor, E.B. (1874). *Primitive Culture: Estes and Lauriat*, London.

Vidyarthi, L.P. and B.K. Rai (1976). *The Tribal Culture of India*, New Delhi: Concept Publishing Company Pvt. Ltd.

Vyas, N.N. (1981). "Tribal and Forest", in N.N. Vyas (Ed.), *Social Forestry in Tribal Development*, Udaipur: MLV Tribal Research Training Institute.

INDEX